Penguin Special
The Concorde Fiasco

Andrew Wilson is an Associate Editor of the *Observer*, for
which he writes on aviation and defence matters. He was born
in Kent in 1923 and attended The Kings School, Canterbury.
After serving in the Second World War as a tank officer he
read Philosophy, Politics, and Economics at Oxford before
joining the *Daily Express* as personal Assistant to Lord
Beaverbrook. From 1953 until joining the *Observer* in 1960
he worked for the BBC. He has written several books, of which
the most recent is *War Gaming*, a study of the misuse of
military planning techniques, published as a Pelican in the
United Kingdom and (under the title *The Bomb and the
Computer*) by the Delacorte Press in the United States. He
was one of the earliest critics of Concorde and has been
frequently quoted – and attacked – in Parliament. In 1972
he was asked to give evidence on Concorde to the Joint
Committee of the United States Congress.
With his wife, a publisher, he lives in Finchley, North London.

The Concorde Fiasco

Andrew Wilson

Penguin Books

With love to
a wonderful
Pythian!

a. W. 16.5.77

Penguin Books Ltd, Harmondsworth,
Middlesex, England
Penguin Books Inc., 7110 Ambassador Road,
Baltimore, Maryland 21207, U.S.A.
Penguin Books Australia Ltd, Ringwood,
Victoria, Australia

First published 1973

Made and printed in Great Britain by
Hunt Barnard Printing Ltd, Aylesbury, Bucks
Set in Monotype Times

Contents

Introduction

Over the years the Concorde supersonic airliner has become the symbol of a special kind of folly in government decision-making. The process begins with a challenging idea, put forward by parties with a professional or commercial interest in its development. The idea meets no particular need but attracts the attention of the Government because it promises technological 'progress' with which most governments – and particularly the technologically ignorant – are anxious to be identified.

If politically opportune, the idea is subjected to a crude form of cost benefit analysis which largely relies, on the cost side at least, on the estimates of those promoting it. The results can then be used to rationalize its adoption which is essentially decided on grounds quite different from those put forward publicly. If later on the costs turn out to be astronomically high, the project is declared to be vital to national prestige. If there are no sales or other visible benefits, it is declared to be rich in technological learning or 'spin off'.

What it never receives is a systematic examination of the priority of its claim on development resources, its impact on the environment, and its value – or non-value – to mankind in general.

In the case of Concorde this process was particularly blatant. But there are other reasons why it deserves special study as a case-history of what was wrong with government decision-making on technology in the 1960s and early 1970s.

The first of these is the secrecy with which it was surrounded.

In 1962 the Anglo–French supersonic programme was re-presented to Parliament as no more than a joint operation that would halve the cost of a project beyond the resources of either Britain or France alone. No one bothered to tell MPs of either the binding nature of the Anglo–French agreement, or the vagueness of the cost estimates, or the disagreements with the French over the design and capacity of the aircraft. Parliament, too, was partly to blame, for failing to inform itself on technical matters. But when MPs later began asking awkward questions about the recovery of the vast public investment, they were given evasive answers or denied information on the specious grounds that disclosure would be commercially damaging. If parliamentary practice had been otherwise – if, for example, the British Government had been obliged to produce information about Concorde in the same way that the American Administration was obliged to answer questions from Congress about the US Supersonic Transport – it is difficult to believe that the waste of public funds would have progressed as far as it did.

The other point on which Concorde deserves special study is the light-hearted way in which the project was begun without any investigation of its effects on the environment. As this book points out, one of these – the boom – was already known and warnings had been given. Others, such as the risk of upper atmosphere pollution, only emerged later. In so far as any of these threats have receded, it is because the Concorde has been a sales flop. But there is unfortunately no sign that the British Government, any more than the French, Russian, Chinese or American Governments, would hesitate for a moment to reactivate them if it saw a chance of selling more aeroplanes.

The exposure of these matters is the purpose of this book, in which I have tried to tell the story of Concorde from the beginning. This includes its technical history as well as the story of miscalculation and pretence over its operating economics, and of the souring of relations between the makers and the customer airlines.

Nobody who has flown in Concorde or watched its construction can fail to be impressed by its engineering. The machinery required to fly passengers at twice the speed of sound, at an altitude of more than 10 miles above the earth, involves an almost incredible degree of ingenuity and complexity. It is also (noise apart) an exceptionally beautiful aeroplane, and I understand those who feel aesthetically towards it as they might towards a Henry Moore sculpture or some other work of art.

I cannot, however, disguise my belief that it was politically irresponsible to start Concorde, wrong to continue it when its failure became apparent, and socially unforgivable to pour more than £1,000 million into a jet-set plaything when the resources were so urgently needed for other tasks.

London, July 1973

A.W.

Acknowledgements

In writing of the political side I have drawn on many sources of information that, for obvious reasons, must stay nameless.

On the technical side I must thank Air Commodore John Davis, whose book *The Concorde Affair* remains the best on the early days of the project, and who was kind enough to talk to me about his material. I am also indebted to colleagues on *Flight International*, *Aviation Week*, and *Interavia* for providing me with a mass of technical data. In the chapter on the American Supersonic Transport I have drawn extensively on C. J. V. Murphy's authoritative article 'Boeing's ordeal with the SST' in *Fortune* magazine of October 1968, and, in the chapter on the Russian Le Bourget disaster, on the *Aviation Week* post mortem. My greatest debts, however, are to the small group of people with whom I have shared the fight against Concorde – Bo Lundberg, former head of the Aeronautical Research Institute of Sweden, Mary Goldring of the *Economist*, and Richard Wiggs and Nigel Haigh of the Anti-Concorde Project.

Figures 1 and 2 are reproduced by kind permission of Squadron-Leader Darrol Stinton and G. T. Foulis and Company, the drawing of the Super-Caravelle in Figure 4 by permission of John Taylor, and the diagrams on pages 127 and 128 by permission of Bo Lundberg.

Finally I must thank Miss Sue Newson-Smith and Miss Linda de Paris for their infinite patience with the typing of the book, and my wife for not complaining at the lost weekends caused by the writing of it.

A.W.

1. Keeping up with America

Interest in a supersonic airliner began in Britain and America in the 1950s. At the time it seemed a logical goal after the launching of the first generation of passenger jets whose leader, the de Havilland Comet, first flew commercially in 1953. In 1939 the best-airliner speed, that of the Douglas DC–3, was 170 m.p.h. By 1946 large four-engined propeller planes were flying at 250 m.p.h. The Comet, soon to be followed by the Boeing 707 and Douglas DC–8, raised the figure to over 500 m.p.h. To make the next step it was necessary to pass the speed of sound which, at the height at which supersonic airliners would fly, was about 650 m.p.h.

There was nothing new about flying faster than sound. Supersonic fighters were already flying with the United States Air Force, and American experimental aircraft had reached speeds of more than 1,500 m.p.h. The challenge lay in constructing a commercial supersonic means of transport with sufficient range and payload to offset its operating costs. Why these were likely to be so high had best be explained at the beginning.

It is a basic fact of flight that a moving aircraft is supported by its wings, which are so shaped as to create more air pressure below than above the wing surfaces. This support is called lift. The aircraft also encounters resistance from the air, known as drag, which much be overcome by thrust from the engines. The ratio of lift to drag determines the plane's aerodynamic efficiency and thus affects its operating economics. In subsonic aircraft an economic ratio is readily attainable. But as soon as an aircraft 'goes supersonic' the drag increases sharply. This is because the plane is no longer preceded by its own sound, which is a vibration of the air and which prepares the air to part at the moment of impact. Without the vibration to warn it, the air, instead of flowing smoothly round the wing, jams tight before the leading surfaces and can be parted only by the creation of a sonic bang. This uses up energy, causes kinetic heating in the skin of the plane, and produces effects on the ground, of which more will be said later.

In military aircraft the problem of supersonic drag, or 'wave drag', was superable. To begin with, it could be reduced by giving the plane a very narrow cross-section, because only the pilot, or the pilot and a second crewman behind him, had to be accommodated. Also military planes could be given extremely powerful and thirsty engines that were used at maximum power for only a part of each mission. The designers of a supersonic airliner were denied these solutions. First, they had to accommodate a large number of passengers in a wide cabin, which also had to be equipped with air-conditioning, galleys, and other amenities. Second, their plane had to be capable of cruising supersonically for most of its flight.

The crux of the problem was fuel. To overcome supersonic drag and to provide the thin-winged plane with sufficient thrust at take-off, the engines had to burn an enormous quantity of kerosene. Lifting so much fuel could necessitate still heavier engines, which in turn could require more fuel, and so on until the spiral ended by reducing the payload to nothing.

This basic design problem was aggravated by another. Up to now nearly all commercial aircraft had been based on experience with military types, and this reduced their research and development costs. But the supersonic transport would be the first of its kind – a 'frontiers-of-knowledge' project in the plane-makers' favourite phrase. Its development would call for the kind of resources that had hitherto been needed only for advanced bomber and fighter aircraft; and because of the high risk of failure, such large sums of money were unlikely to be obtainable from the private sector of the economy.

The arguments by which the British and French Governments were persuaded to spend vast sums on behalf of their taxpayers are the themes of later chapters. But it may here be observed that in the 1950s, when the idea of Concorde started, technological progress was held in unquestioning esteem. Jet airliners were a novelty and an object of wonder. Airports, with their glitter and roar, were shrines to the future; and there were people living near them who could still hear the sound of big Boeing 707s with a touch of civic pride. The jets of course were only one feature of the technological landscape then marvellously unfolding. But for the man-in-the-street they encouraged a belief, akin to the earlier faith of the Victorian Steam Age, in technology's ability to enrich the world by shrinking it.

In addition to this uncritical optimism, which was almost universal, there was, in Britain and in France, a separate and decisive influence at work.

For many years Britain – to the belief of most Britons – had led the world in aeronautical progress. It was British engineers who, on the eve of the Second World War, had produced the Hurricane and Spitfire fighters. It was British scientists who had changed the whole character of air warfare by inventing radar. More important still, it was an Englishman, Group-Captain Frank Whittle, who had invented the jet engine which first took to the air in 1941. But when America entered the war in December that year it was agreed that Britain should concentrate on fighter production, leaving America to build heavy bombers for the daylight bombardment of Germany and Japan. This division of tasks meant that, when the war ended, the US had ready an industrial base for the large-scale production of four-engined airliners, whereas Britain had to start almost from scratch with factories whose experience was chiefly in the making of single-engined fighters.

Foreseeing this problem back in 1943 Mr Churchill's government had set up the Brabazon committee on post-war aviation. When the war ended, the committee's proposals led to two major projects: an eight-engined airliner, the Bristol Brabazon, and a ten-engined flying boat, the Saunders-Roe Princess. These two aircraft were supposed to give British Overseas Airways Corporation the last word in luxury planes, with sleeping berths, dining saloons, and all the potted-palm spaciousness of pre-war air travel. Both were ignominiously cancelled when it was belatedly realized that the post-war market was for functional airliners using the 10,000-foot concrete runways that had been built the world over for military use. The Brabazon was scrapped in 1952 having cost £6.5 million and the Princess two years later after three prototypes had been built costing £9 million.

Not every post-war project was so ludicrously misconceived (the turbo-propeller Viscount, begun in 1946 and put into service in 1953, sold 438 copies). But a series of other flops – including the Avro Tudor, which had to be withdrawn after two disappeared without trace over the South Atlantic – destroyed all hope of challenging the Americans in the market for long-haul piston-engined planes. It thus fell to de Havillands to attempt to defeat the American goliath with a design that showed a dramatic advance in both speed and comfort: the jet Comet.

The Comet both anticipated and influenced the Concorde in a number of ways. Like Concorde it was a beautifully shaped aeroplane incorporating simultaneous new departures in both engines and airframe (a combination that raises safety questions). It was also under-ranged and somewhat small. It could not fly the Atlantic non-stop, and this gravely curtailed its sales prospects; and it could carry only 85 passengers compared with a payload of 140 or more being planned for the intercontinental Boeing 707. These early shortcomings might have been overcome, however, but for a disastrous mistake in its construction.

Almost on the anniversary of its entry into service a Comet crashed near Calcutta. An inquiry found that the structure had given way in a thunder squall. Eight months later, in January 1954, another Comet fell out of the sky near Elba. Little could be recovered from the deep water, and flights were resumed after precautionary modifications. A third crash occurred on 8 April, when a Comet on charter to South African Airways plunged into the sea near Naples. The entire fleet was grounded and in the course of a lengthy investigation a complete Comet fuselage was put through pressure tests in a specially constructed water tank. These revealed a fatigue failure in the paper-thin fuselage skin at the corner of a window. The tests and the subsequent re-design of the Comet took nearly three years. By the time it was ready to re-enter service Britain's lead in jet design had been lost to the Boeing 707 and Douglas DC–8. Only 77 Comets were ultimately sold for commercial service – a fraction of the run that had been hoped for.

The Comet disaster might reasonably have discouraged the

British aircraft industry from ever again attempting a radically new design with which it stood to make costly mistakes while the larger American industry benefited by the lessons. But the compulsive desire to 'get even' with the Americans dictated otherwise. It was not the Comet's failure that stuck in British minds, but the bad luck that had robbed it of success. Though few in the industry would have put it so directly, the Concorde became Britain's means of avenging the Comet – only this time there must be no mistakes in the structural engineering.

At this period, in the early 1950s, a small band of supersonic enthusiasts was to be found at the Royal Aircraft Establishment, Farnborough. 'Farnborough', as it is more simply called, holds a central place in British aviation. It is the chief establishment for government-funded aerospace research, and its laboratories and workshops are equipped for almost anything, from fundamental research into the properties of metals to the structural testing of complete aircraft. At Farnborough the supersonic project became a practical possibility due mainly to the efforts of three men – the Deputy Director, Morien Morgan; the Director of Supersonic Research, Philip Hufton; and a German engineer called Dietrich Küchemann who, before coming to RAE in 1946, had designed advanced fighters for the German Luftwaffe.

In 1955 Morgan, Hufton, and Küchemann persuaded the Establishment to set up a working party on supersonic transport. This produced the discouraging finding that a plane with thin wings, a slender fuselage, and a weight of about 340,000lb. might indeed be feasible, but that due to supersonic drag it would be able to carry only 18 passengers between London and New York. As this would have meant paying a fare of several thousand pounds, the matter was dropped. But before the end of the year Hufton had another try.

In October he went to the United States for talks with experts in military aircraft design. In a series of tests with wind-tunnel models the Americans had found that drag could be minimized if an aircraft presented the same area of cross-section throughout its length. Though this applied strictly to conditions at Mach 1,* the discovery might be used to reduce drag at slightly higher speeds. When Hufton returned to Farnborough he

* The speed of sound, called after the Austrian physicist, Ernst Mach.

revived interest in supersonics by proposing a design that would cruise at Mach 1.2.

At the same time Dietrich Küchemann became interested in the idea of applying the 'delta' wing-shape, used for Britain's subsonic V-bombers, to a supersonic airliner. The delta, he said, could be used to reduce wave drag by an effect called 'separated flow'. In a condition of separated flow the aircraft was supported not by the smooth airflow over the wing surface, as in the subsonic aircraft, but by contrived eddies of air *below* the wing.

In the winter of 1955–6 Morgan, Hufton, and Küchemann discussed the question with the Director of Farnborough, George Gardiner. Together they decided that the next step should be not another Farnborough working party, but a full-scale inquiry by all interested parties in government and the industry. Gardiner lobbied ministers, airframe and engine firms, and senior civil servants. After six months he won. The Government agreed to finance an inquiry into all aspects of building a supersonic vehicle.

The Supersonic Transport Aircraft Committee began work in November 1956. It included representatives of the main airframe and engine companies, the two state airlines – BOAC and BEA – the Air Registration Board, government research establishments, the Ministry of Aviation, the Ministry of Supply, and, of course, RAE itself. Morgan headed the main committee, which met about once a month, leaving Hufton and Küchemann to do detailed and continuous work on a technical committee. Specialized sub-committees were appointed to deal with subsonic and supersonic aerodynamics, engines, airline operation, and other aspects.

It has been argued that the Supersonic Transport Aircraft Committee, including as it did some of the ablest brains in the industry, was a model of what scientists and technologists could achieve in cooperation. This is a fair statement as to its technical investigations, though, as we shall see, it quite failed to comprehend (or at least to acknowledge) the economic pitfalls of the supersonic project.

The main question facing the committee was what should be the speed of the supersonic transport. On the basis of the available technology this could be at a variety of points between Mach 1 and Mach 3. At the lower end of the scale there were arguments for an aircraft that would cruise at about Mach 1.2. Although this was only 200 m.p.h. faster than the subsonic Boeing 707, it had the advantage that up to Mach 1.2 it is possible by aerodynamic tricks to avoid producing a sonic bang. Also a Mach 1.2 plane would be almost as good as a faster aircraft on medium-haul routes where the advantage of higher speeds was reduced by the time taken for take-off, climb-out, and landing.

But looking at the long-haul market, if one exceeded Mach 1.2 and believed that a sonic bang would be acceptable, it made sense to build the fastest plane possible. In this case the design speed would be determined by the choice of construction materials, and vice versa, because of the behaviour of different types of metal when kinetically heated.

Due to the kinetic effect, the temperature of an aircraft skin increases logarithmically in relation to its speed. Thus at Mach 2 it is about 100 degrees Centigrade, and at Mach 3 nearly 300 degrees. But at 100 degrees aluminium alloys, the metal chiefly used in conventional aircraft, begin to lose their strength. Therefore if an aircraft is to be subjected to skin temperatures higher than 100 degrees it must be built of titanium or some other expensive material which retains its strength in a wide variety of conditions.

Faced with the choice between aluminium for Mach 2 or titanium for a higher speed (which would also have meant installing complex systems for cooling the fuel and cabin atmosphere) the Supersonic Transport Committee considered how each type of supersonic aircraft would perform in service over the North Atlantic, which was considered the supersonic transport's best market.

When they looked at possible flight schedules the advantages of flying much faster than Mach 2 seemed to be small. For example, flying at Mach 2.6 – which was thought to be the optimum speed for a titanium plane – would only cut the London—New York flight time to 2 hours 30 minutes. This was barely half an hour less than the flight time of a Mach 2 aircraft. From the airline's point of view what mattered most was that, because of noise restrictions on night-time operations at airports and the refusal of passengers to fly at awkward hours, the faster plane could make only four transatlantic crossings a day, the same number as the Mach 2 aircraft.

Such were the grounds on which the Committee decided in favour of aluminium, though they cautiously proposed a speed of Mach 1.8 rather than Mach 2 because not enough was yet known about the effect of repeated temperature changes on aluminium near its maximum permissible heat.

The second major question to be decided by the Committee was the capacity of the aircraft. Here they proved slightly more realistic than the later constructors of the Concorde, for they calculated that the long-range aircraft would need to have 150 seats in order to compete on operating costs with subsonic aircraft such as the Boeing 707. For the medium-range aircraft they proposed only 100 seats, arguing that the smaller plane could provide more frequent services.

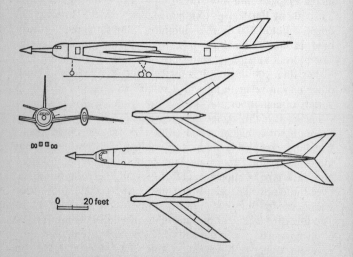

Figure 1. The M-wing.

Finally there was the question of shape. A basic feature of every supersonic design is the sharp sweeping back of the wings and leading edges in order to reduce drag. For the proposed Mach 1.2 plane the experts came up with the so-called M-wing design (Figure 1), in which the wings were swept back about 60 degrees from engines mounted in the middle of each wing. Strange though it may look from the drawing, the M-wing promised greater rigidity than a simple sweep back from the fuselage. But it soon became clear that the design which most interested the Committee was the Mach 2 long-range plane.

For this the Committee chose a delta wing that would generate Küchemann's detached airflow. It was the obvious shape. But using it, two different outlines were possible. One was a dart-shaped but conventional aircraft with a separate wing and fuselage. The other was an 'integrated' design in which a separate fuselage was dispensed with and the crew and passengers were carried in the wing itself. In the end the Committee chose the integrated design which, had it been carried

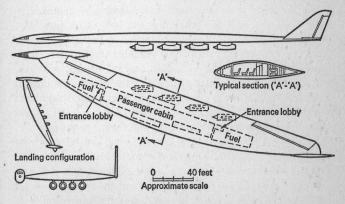

Figure 2. In 1961 Handley Page proposed this 'slewed wing' design for speeds around Mach 2. The wing contained the passengers and could be slewed in relation to the crew cabin at one tip, the fin and rudder at the other, and the engines in between. For low speeds it would be flown at right angles to the direction of flight; at supersonic speeds it would be sharply swept back, like one wing of a swing-wing plane. It was expected to yield up to 20 per cent better lift/drag ratios than a Concorde-type slender delta. The trouble was the complexity of its mechanics.

21

through, would have made the Concorde a truly revolutionary aircraft. As we shall see, the decision was reversed. But first it was necessary to solve a critical problem surrounding the delta wing and supersonic operations as a whole.

Because of some early experiments in the United States, it had long been supposed that delta wings caused hazards on landing; that for aerodynamic reasons they had to be landed at a steep angle; and that because of this they were liable to be rolled over by cross-winds. An American report said the danger began at an angle of 3 degrees, well below the 15-degree angle at which the supersonic airliner would need to land on existing runways. The problem was investigated by a remarkable personality at Farnborough, W. E. Gray.

Gray, an ex-First World War fighter pilot and freelance inventor who had entered the Royal Aircraft Establishment without a scientific degree, mistrusted the American report and decided to establish the facts for himself. By the expedient of launching wooden models from a step-ladder he managed to show that, although the delta wing was subject to instability, this did not occur until the wing reached angles much greater than those suggested. He further established that the wing's instability was a function of the ratio of its span to its length, and that if the span was two thirds of the length, the critical angle would be over 25 degrees. Farnborough aerodynamicists confirmed Gray's findings in wind-tunnel tests, and the critical objection to the delta wing was in due course removed.

In March 1959, after nearly two and a half years' study, the Supersonic Transport Aircraft Committee reported to the Ministry of Aviation. It recommended the development of *two* aircraft – a Mach 1.8 design for long range, and a Mach 1.2 for short range. It did not rule out the technical feasibility of a Mach 2.6 design but questioned its advantages and said such a design would take too long to develop. It also ruled out two other developments – a swing-wing design and a vertical take-off design – on the grounds that they were too complex to embark on at this stage.

In making these recommendations the Committee avoided the worst of the follies which later marked the American Supersonic Transport (SST) programme. But they erred on three points. The first was the capacity of the aircraft, which was still too small to compete with subsonic planes of the next generation. The second was the sonic boom, whose social implications they simply ignored. The third was the cost, which they grossly underestimated at £90 million for the long-range plane, and £50–70 million for the medium-range one.

2. The Supersonic Caravelle

Hopes of selling the supersonic airliner depended on gaining a lead over the Americans who, notwithstanding their early doubt about the stability of the delta wing, had begun theoretical studies at about the same time. In September 1959 the Ministry of Aviation commissioned two firms to make feasibility studies in the Mach 2 range. The Bristol Aeroplane Company, which has just become part of the British Aircraft Corporation, was asked to study a delta wing design with a conventional separate fuselage. The new Hawker Siddeley company, which had absorbed de Havillands, was asked to study the Supersonic Transport Aircraft Committee's preferred all-wing shape. This caused comment because Hawker Siddeley had less supersonic experience than BAC and was regarded as the less favoured candidate in any competition for a development contract. What had happened was that the experts had had second thoughts about the all-wing shape and were harking back to a separate fuselage design.

Unexpectedly, in addition to the Mach 2 study, both firms were asked to study the feasibility of a Mach 2.7 aircraft. This was a type the Committee had said should be left to the distant future. The second type of plane the Committee had proposed, the Mach 1.2, was quietly dropped. This was on the grounds, hardly contestable, that Britain could not afford to develop two supersonic transports at once, and that the Mach 1.2, being for medium-range operations only, would have the smaller market. Six months later the studies of the Mach 2.7 plane were also ended, both companies having reported that it would be much heavier than the Mach 2 and would have double the production and operating costs.

It was now up to the Government, advised by its experts at Farnborough and elsewhere, to decide between the integrated shape and the separate fuselage. The chief drawback of the former was the thickness of wing required to accommodate passengers. In a 100-seat aircraft, the biggest Hawker Siddeley found feasible within the weight limit set by the Ministry of Aviation, this produced poor aerodynamic qualities, although some experts believed that it would be the right shape for a larger plane. Another factor favouring the conventional shape was a shift which occurs in the aerodynamic centre of an aircraft when it goes supersonic and which can most easily be balanced when passengers are seated well forward in a long cabin. A further point in favour of the separate fuselage was simply the manufacturers' long experience with its construction. All these points having been endorsed by the feasibility studies, in July 1960 the Minister of Aviation, Peter Thorneycroft, announced his decision. BAC was to be given a £350,000 contract for a 'limited design study' of a plane with a separate fuselage. It was to be capable of carrying 120 passengers at a speed of Mach 2.2 – a slightly higher Mach number than previously envisaged, because of improved knowledge about the behaviour of aluminium.

The award of the contract to BAC put Hawker Siddeley out of the competition – a fact they first learned from the newspapers.

BAC took a year to complete the design study. During this time the supersonic aircraft increased its capacity to 130 passengers and its all-up weight to 380,000lb. (about 170 tons). The design was called the Bristol 198 and used six engines. This was a questionable arrangement because problems arise with the air intake of the centre engine in a bank of three. Nor was the Ministry of Aviation happy about the weight which, on the basis of military experience, was bound to lead to an increase in development costs. Even before the design was submitted, therefore, the Government asked BAC to study a smaller, four-engined plane, capable of crossing the Atlantic with about 100 passengers. This was to have an all-up weight of 250,000lb. and was designated the BAC–223. But, once again, before the new study could be completed a new development occurred – this time severely affecting the British initiative.

In June 1961 the French firm, Sud Aviation, announced a

supersonic transport design that bore a strong resemblance to British efforts but weighed less than 200,000lb.

Behind the French design lay a curious episode. In 1959 members of the staff of ONERA, the French equivalent of Farnborough, had paid a visit to the Royal Aircraft Establishment, in the course of which they discussed the problems of a supersonic transport. This was something that interested the French as keenly as the British, and for much the same reasons, including a desire to get even with the Americans. The Supersonic Transport Aircraft Committee was then completing its report, and its findings were secret. But RAE members were authorized to tell their guests that they believed a supersonic transport might be technically and commercially feasible. The French remained sceptical, however, having themselves encountered the stability problem with delta wings and having tried unsuccessfully to overcome it by fitting a small foreplane or canard.

But when a year later RAE members paid a return visit to ONERA they found a different view prevailing. Not only did the French now consider a supersonic airliner feasible, they even produced designs that were uncannily similar to the delta wing proposed in the British committee's report. What had happened, quite simply, was that someone had sent them a copy of the report.

Now the STAC report covered two years' research which foreign aviation interests would have given much to know about. In particular it contained the results of Gray's Farnborough experiments with delta wing models. Using a curiously exact phrase, the Ministry of Aviation had stamped it 'For British Eyes Only' – and even today its contents have not been divulged to Parliament.

Who sent the report? Though this too remains a secret, his name is known in Whitehall and he appears to have been highly placed. His motives were doubtless honourable, grounded in the belief that French collaboration was necessary for a supersonic programme. But the consequences of the action were extremely serious.

As soon as the French read the report they knew that the supersonic drag problem could be solved by delta wing, and within eighteen months they were to become Britain's equals in the Concorde project. Through the disclosure of two years' secrets, Britain forfeited design leadership while France, obsessed with the desire to build an instant, medium-range, and too small aircraft, was able to destroy whatever slim chance the project had at the outset.

Shortly after the British visit to ONERA, M. Georges Hereil, Vice-Chairman of Sud Aviation, announced that his firm and its rival, Dassault, were jointly engaged on a supersonic design that could be flying in 1964. He said it would probably be delta-winged, have a range of 2,500 miles, and could be powered with either British or American engines. The two firms were prepared to collaborate internationally on a long-range version, but were determined to develop the medium-range one entirely within France. Vague though this sounded, a year later M. Hereil announced that a prototype was to be built and that the plane would enter service in 1967–8. This was the design that now emerged to compete with the British. It was presented at the Paris Air Show in June 1961 under the name 'Super-Caravelle'.*

Whatever its genesis the Super-Caravelle appeared at a politically convenient moment. At the end of 1960 the British Prime Minister, Harold Macmillan, had decided on a major change in British foreign policy. Deserting the idea of a seven-nation European Free Trade Area, he decided that Britain should join the European Economic Community, which it had declined to enter six years earlier. In July 1961, a few weeks after the Sud Aviation announcement, he told Parliament that the Government intended to apply for Community membership; and in October the British and European Governments, led by France, began formal negotiations.

One of Macmillan's leading 'Europeans' was the Minister of Aviation, Peter Thorneycroft. A former Chancellor of the Exchequer who had resigned over economic policy, Thorneycroft had been invited back into government as part of Macmillan's switch to the Six. Everyone knew that Britain's chances of joining the Six depended on the goodwill of President de

---

* Not to be confused with later versions of the *sub*sonic Caravelle, which were given the same name.

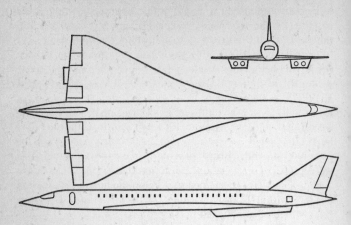

Figure 3. Proposed outline for the Super-Caravelle.

Gaulle; and to Thorneycroft, Anglo–French collaboration in aerospace seemed the obvious way to establish a preparatory entente. For this reason he quickly enlisted the help of his opposite number, the French Minister of Transport, M. Robert Buron, in instigating a dialogue between BAC and Sud Aviation.

Although the two firms were collaborating on some smaller projects, neither at this stage showed any inclination for a supersonic partnership. BAC knew that its long-range design required a great deal more work to be done on it, while Sud took the line that it could get on quite well by itself with a medium-range prototype. Talks got no further than the possible sharing of engines and some airframe parts. Buron then suggested a ministerial meeting, which was held in September and ended with himself and Thorneycroft proclaiming the wastefulness of separate designs and ordering the companies to study one type of aircraft with a medium- and a long-range version.

Three months later they reported back, but with totally different suggestions. BAC proposed medium- and long-range versions of its own plane, the Bristol 223, with all-up weights of 228,000lb. and 255,000lb. respectively. Sud proposed medium- and long-range versions of the Super-Caravelle with weights of 203,000lb. and 241,00lb. Almost the only thing common to the two designs was their capacity – 100 seats in the medium-range version and 90 in the long-range version.

The fact was that the French were determined to build a medium-range plane that might later be adapted to long range, while the British were set on a long-range plane that might be adapted to medium range. The French thought the medium-range aircraft should be built quickly, leaving the long-range market to engage the Americans. The British knew that it was easier to produce a medium-range plane from a long-range plane than vice versa and that the Americans, once they got going, would not neglect the medium-range market for long.

Thorneycroft and Buron again ordered the companies to produce a joint outline. But they had still not done so when the Ministers held their next meeting in March 1962.

Pressure now came from the political summit. For 9 months the talks on Britain's Common Market entry had proceeded fitfully because of Anglo–French differences over the Community's political and economic goals. But in June Macmillan and de Gaulle had an unexpectedly cordial meeting at the Château de Champs, near Paris. So encouraging was the encounter that Macmillan returned to London determined to make Common Market membership the central theme of the Conservative Party conference in October, and possibly of an autumn general election. The supersonic transport agreement was thus needed urgently as a means of affirming the new Anglo–French partnership.

Under increased pressure BAC and Sud Aviation finally agreed to unveil what passed for a joint design at the Farnborough Air Show in September. After thirteen months of talking it was still no more than a file of publicity material and a painted model; but three weeks later they presented their Governments with a 14-page brochure showing that the plane was to have a 220,000lb., 100-seat, medium-range version and a 262,000lb., 90-seat, long-range one.

On 29 October, still under governmental pressure, the companies signed an agreement for joint development and production. The arrangements were unprecedented in sacrificing economy to the principle of exactly equal work sharing. There were to be separate production lines at Bristol and Toulouse, at which centres each partner would assemble complete aircraft in addition to providing its share of parts and assemblies for the common programme. BAC would make the nose and tail of the aircraft, and Sud Aviation the middle part of the fuselage and the wings. A similar division would be made in the supply of components for the electrical, hydraulic, and fuel systems, which involved the work of hundreds of sub-contractors. Work on the power plant was to be shared under a separate agreement signed by the engine companies a few days later. The engine itself – the Bristol Siddeley Olympus 593 – was to be made at Bristol, leaving the French national engine firm, SNECMA, to make the complex air intakes and the rest of the assembly at Villacoubay, near Paris. The arrangement gave Britain about 60 per cent of the engine work, and France about 60 per cent of the airframe work. It also added about 10 per cent to the cost because of the expense of shipping components from one country to another.

The signing of the commercial agreements cleared the way for the Government-to-Government agreement that was to set the seal on Anglo–French technological cooperation.

The document itself was not very long. It had only to provide, in the most general terms, for the definition of the aircraft, the equal sharing of responsibility for its development, and a means of supervising the work. Yet by this the two Governments saddled themselves with an albatross.

Article 1 specified that there should be equal sharing of work and expenditure by the two Governments, who would also share the proceeds of sales. Article 4 provided for the setting up of 'integrated organizations of the airframe and engine firms'.

Article 6 provided for a standing committee of British and French officials to supervise progress, report to their Governments, and make appropriate proposals.

But the most astounding thing about the agreement was what it omitted. There was no provision for either country to withdraw if it decided that the supersonic transport project was not worth continuing for economic or technical reasons.

This absence of an escape clause was not just an oversight. It was a deliberate act of policy *on the British side*.

Three factors appear to have contributed to the Government's decision on this point. First, it believed that a project so immense and complex could be contemplated only on the basis of a total commitment by both partners. Second, it was afraid that the French might later pull out and build a plane of their own with the accumulated know-how. Third, some Ministers felt that the irrevocable commitment – a kind of 'blood pact' – was needed to allay French suspicions of 'perfidious Albion'.

The agreement was finally signed on 29 November 1962 at Lancaster House in London. Due to last-minute complications in Paris it was impossible to get the signature of a French Minister. It was therefore signed on the French side by the French Ambassador, M. Geoffroy de Courcel, and on the British by Thorneycroft's successor, Julian Amery. Thus did the two Governments commit themselves to finance, entirely from public funds and without any financial liability by the manufacturers, the most costly civil technological enterprise in the Western world.

On the day of the signing, the British Government let it be known in Washington that it expected Britain to be a member of the European Community within twelve months. In London Amery said that steps had been taken to control the costs and keep Britain's share to £75–85 million. The agreement itself was deposited with the International Court at the Hague, which gave it the status of a treaty.

For the next six weeks the Macmillan Government continued to believe that it had bought French support for its entry into Europe – a belief undimmed by any realization of the political consequences of the Nassau agreement which gave Britain Polaris in place of the cancelled Skybolt programme or of French hostility to the Anglo–American relationship.

On Monday 14 January de Gaulle launched his own Skybolt at a dramatically contrived press conference in the Elysée.

Britain, he told the 800 reporters, was not yet able to accept the European Community 'without reserve'. It was therefore probable that negotiations might not succeed. As an alternative to membership he held out the possibility of 'associate' status. But de Gaulle knew, as everyone knew, that this was unacceptable, and that for the foreseeable future he was slamming the door in Britain's face. But this was not all. By a brilliant stroke he simultaneously tied Britain to continue with the supersonic project by making it the touchstone of her sincerity in any later application to join Europe. 'Nothing,' he said, 'will prevent our close relationship and direct cooperation, as the two countries have proved by deciding to build together the supersonic aircraft, Concorde.'

It was the first time the name Concorde had been publicly uttered. De Gaulle, without warning his advisers, was using a name that had originally been suggested by the 10-year-old son of a BAC official but had been turned down by French officials as unexciting.

During the troubled months that followed, Macmillan and his successor, Sir Alec Douglas-Home, must have desperately wished to be rid of Concorde. The Treasury did not want it and even the Aviation Ministry was uncomfortably aware that it had assented to the agreement without any means of checking the manufacturers' cost estimates. But because of de Gaulle's diplomacy and the absence of an escape clause, the Government was in no position to get out. Concord (as it was still spelt by the British) had started on the course which was to end in the squandering of hundreds of millions of pounds.

3. A Question of Capacity

The design approved by the British and French Governments on 11 November 1962 was no more than an outline, a deliberately vague compromise agreed on after months of haggling in order to permit the announcement of a politically opportune venture. No sooner had the agreement been signed than Anglo–French differences came out into the open again.

The French, who had much less experience of building advanced aircraft than the British, were impatient to start immediately on detailed drawings. They insisted that the outline design was the basis of a prototype, and that this should be flown as quickly as possible to gain information on supersonic flight problems. Necessary changes could then be made in the production aircraft.

The British, though no less anxious to establish a lead over the Americans, adopted a policy of 'more haste, less speed'. They saw it as an initial design study, the starting point for research into more efficient variants, into the design of systems (whose details had yet to be agreed), and into methods of construction. To start too quickly on the prototype, they said, would lead to delays later on. As far as possible the prototype should resemble the production aircraft.

A major point at issue was the shape of the wing. The French were content to settle for the shape as it was, on the basis of tests in their wind tunnels. But the British mistrusted the French tests, which had been made with relatively crude equipment. They wanted more tests, with more sophisticated wind tunnels – a reasonable demand in view of the fact that even a minor design fault could affect the plane's range by several hundred miles.

Finally, there was a difference of opinion over the size of the aircraft. The Anglo–French agreement had provided for two

CF–3

sizes: a medium-range plane carrying 100 passengers, with an all-up weight of 220,000lb.; and a long-range version carrying 90 passengers, with an all-up weight of 262,000lb. The French, whose Super-Caravelle of 1961 had a planned capacity of 70–80 seats, were quite content with the agreed seating figures. But the British were having doubts about them after discussion with airlines.

The airlines' position on Concorde was difficult. From the start they were cool towards an aircraft that, even if it proved profitable to fly, would involve them in heavy capital expenditure for the second time in less than a decade. (In 1962 they were still recovering from the heavy outlay on the first generation of subsonic jets.) They were therefore careful not to say anything that might be construed as committing them to take the plane. On the other hand both BOAC and BEA had been represented on the Supersonic Transport Aircraft Committee and could not refuse an opinion, even if they had wished, on the design that finally emerged.

As a result of talks with BOAC and other long-range airlines in 1962–3 BAC came to realize that the 90-seat, long-range version was too small, that to cover its operating costs it would need more seats, and that to meet safety requirements it would have to carry more fuel for diversions. It was also persuaded (as was Sud Aviation finally) that the medium-range version was a non-starter. Not only were the supersonic time-savings on medium-range journeys less significant than those on longer ones because of the long climb to supersonic cruising altitude, but it was now realized that objections might be raised concerning the overland sonic booms.

The French, who were still thinking on the lines of the Super-Caravelle, continued to favour the small-capacity aircraft. But by the autumn of 1963, with the agreement one year old and a decision on a prototype design imperative, BAC and the Ministry of Aviation were driven to insist that the capacity be increased to 118 passengers and the payload to 26,000lb., giving an all-up weight of 326,000lb. This meant an increase in engine thrust, which could only be obtained by a major re-design of the Olympus 593 engine.

At this point a word should be said about the Olympus, whose noisy design was to be one of Concorde's main problems.

Oddly enough, the Supersonic Transport Aircraft Committee had made no recommendation about an engine type, though it included representatives of the leading engine-makers, Rolls–Royce and Bristol Siddeley, who knew that the basic type of turbojet engine – of which the Olympus was an example – would present a great noise problem if used to power a supersonic airliner.

The Olympus had been designed for the TSR–2 bomber being developed for the RAF. Both BAC and Hawker Siddeley had adopted it in their early feasibility studies as an alternative to another turbojet, the Rolls-Royce RB 167, because of its great thrust.

It is now clear that a better alternative would have been a by-pass or 'fan jet' engine, the type now fitted to most big subsonic aircraft. The fan jet is not only quieter but (at subsonic speed) much more economical on fuel. In 1961–2, however, it was rejected by the airframe makers on the grounds that its large diameter would present aerodynamic problems in a supersonic aircraft. In 1961 the Olympus was adopted both for the BAC–223 and by the French for their Super-Caravelle. This made its adoption for Anglo–French supersonic transport virtually certain. Only one voice dissented – that of the National Gas Turbine Establishment. Aware of the turbojet noise problem, this recommended a development programme to see if the problems of the by-pass engine could not be overcome. But in the haste to get the supersonic project under way, its advice was ignored.

In November 1963 Bristol Siddeley agreed to increase the thrust of the Olympus from 29,000lb. to 32,825lb. The re-design itself was no problem, but the argument with the French Government and plane-makers dragged on for another five months. It was not until March 1964 that the new capacity was settled, and airlines told about it at a meeting of the technical committee of the International Air Transport Association in Beirut. As we shall see, this was far from being the end of the matter. But before the plane's size again came into question, there was a much more sensational Anglo–French confrontation.

The Concorde had been launched in 1962 by a Conservative Government bent on securing Anglo–French political partnership in Europe. The project had not then been criticized by the Labour Opposition which saw no advantage in attacking a major source of employment in the aircraft industry. But in 1963 Labour Party leaders began to suspect the aerospace industry of deliberately underestimating development costs in order to get government contracts. The outstanding example was the TSR–2 bomber whose development had been started in 1957 at an estimated cost of £90 million. By 1963 the figure had trebled and was to rise to the astronomical sum of £650 million.

From 1963 onward TSR–2 was relentlessly attacked by Denis Healey, the shadow Defence Minister, while the industry as a whole came in for the attention of the Party's aviation committee, under its chairman, Fred Lee. Although the Committee had no power to frame future government policy, it wielded some influence in the Labour Party. Another actor in aviation matters was the redoubtable Col (later Lord) Wigg who had the ear of the Party leader, Mr Wilson. It was Wigg who introduced the shadow Cabinet to the writings of the commercial aviation consultant, Richard Worcester.

Worcester had no party affiliation, but was interested, to quote him, 'in pointing the way to more efficient activity in the aerospace industry'. He had become a consultant after wartime flying in the Fleet Air Arm and a spell of writing for *American Aviation* magazine. In addition to advising clients he published a weekly analysis of aviation developments, which regularly raised the hackles of the British aviation industry because of its sceptical treatment of most British projects.

In November 1963, about the time that Wigg brought him to the attention of Party colleagues, Worcester used his weekly aviation summary to ask some provocative questions about Concorde: Was the industry competent to handle the project? Had the British and French Governments a clear enough idea of the total eventual cost? Could the project gain a sufficient lead to keep the initiative against foreign competition, including a possible Russian plane? Would Concorde be operable by airlines?

At this time the Labour Party was acutely conscious of its ignorance of technical matters. Worcester helped to enlighten it, particularly by pointing out the extravagance of government plans for the simultaneous development of four major aircraft:

Concorde, TSR-2, the HS.681 military transport, and the P-1154 vertical take-off fighter. But he would be the first to disclaim any major responsibility for activating opposition to Concorde. This was the work of the Swedish aircraft designer and safety expert, Bo Lundberg.

In 1961 Lundberg, then head of Sweden's Aeronautical Research Institute, had drawn attention to some problems of supersonic flying in the *New Scientist* (quoted in Chapter 6). Two years later, in August 1963, he returned to the attack with a series of longer articles in the *Observer*. He began by listing the hazards of a plane that would introduce a host of radically new features – in engines, wings, fuselage, materials – for which there was for once very little military experience. He pointed out that the supersonic transport would operate at exceptional altitude and in little-known atmospheric conditions. Its speed meant that pilots could not rely on eyesight to detect weather conditions, some of which, such as hail (which can be present in clouds up to 75,000 feet), could have fatal consequences. Another hazard facing the supersonic airliner was structural fatigue caused by kinetic heating.

But the biggest problem mentioned by Lundberg was the sonic boom. This, he explained, would follow the supersonic transport in a continuous 'carpet' varying from 25 to 100 miles in width according to the plane's weight and altitude. It would produce effects varying from annoyance to severe physical shock, as well as breaking windows and doing structural damage to property. If supersonic flying became widespread, the globe would become bandaged with 'boom carpets' – an intolerable price for ordinary people to pay for the transportation of privileged business travellers.

In January 1964 the fears for the environment aroused by Lundberg's warnings were joined by suspicions about Concorde's financial management as the result of a report by the House of Commons Estimates Committee. They discovered that the Treasury, which was supposed to be the tax-payer's 'watchdog', had been sleeping on the Concorde programme. It had taken no part in the preparation of the Anglo–French supersonic transport agreement; nor had it consulted with the French Ministry of Finance on the project; nor was it represented on the committee of officials supervising the financing of Concorde. The committee made two highly critical recommendations: actual and estimated expenditure should in future be clearly identifiable in estimates laid before Parliament, and the Treasury should be continuously informed of progress in order to advise Ministers. As a result control was tightened, but no improvement could undo the consequences of the initial mistake about the size of the plane.

In July the development cost estimate of £150–170 million was raised to £280 million. This was to cover the increase in size and payload agreed with the makers in May. The announcement was followed soon afterwards by a disclosure that the unit cost of the aircraft was expected to be £5 million – an increase of £1½ million on the figure quoted two years before. Even to the Conservative Government, which had seen large increases in cost estimates for its military projects, this increase must have given food for thought. It was not made more palatable by the worsening of Anglo–French relations that had followed the Nassau pact.

In the meantime there had been two other developments. The first was the commencement of work on the American Supersonic Transport (SST). Following a decision to go for a Mach 3 type of aircraft the National Aeronautics and Space Administration had in 1963 awarded short-term design-study contracts to three airframe companies: Boeing and Lockheed, which both had extensive civil experience, and North American Aviation, which had built the B–70 supersonic bomber. Similar contracts had been given to the three major engine companies: General Electric, Pratt and Whitney, and Curtiss-Wright. In July 1964 the Administration awarded further short-term study contracts to Boeing and Lockheed on airframes, and to General Electric and Pratt and Whitney on engines. President Kennedy had meanwhile announced a supersonic programme with an expenditure ceiling of $750 million, that envisaged the SST being ready for service in 1971 – only a year after Concorde.

The other, less noticed, development was the commencement of work on a Soviet supersonic transport. Rumour had it that it was merely a 'civilianized' version of the Blinder supersonic bomber; and anyone suggesting that the Soviet plane, looking very much like Concorde, might be the first to fly would have been ridiculed.

4. Labour's About-Face

On Thursday 15 October 1964 the Labour Party won the general election with a majority of five seats. Its victory was confirmed about 3 p.m. on Friday. At 4 p.m. Mr Wilson drove to the Palace and by early evening had picked his chief Ministers. Of these, two were of immediate consequence to the aircraft industry – George Brown, head of the new Department of Economic Affairs, and James Callaghan, the Chancellor of the Exchequer.

In his book, *The First 100 Days of Harold Wilson*, Anthony Shrimsley has described how Callaghan was immediately told of the full extent of Britain's economic crisis. As he emerged from accepting office he was met by the Chancellor's private secretary who told him that the head of the Treasury, Sir William Armstrong, was waiting next door in No. 11 Downing Street and would like to discuss the economic situation.

Bancroft [the secretary] escorted Callaghan along the connecting corridor to the ground floor study of the Chancellor's official residence . . . where Armstrong stood with his senior officials. They sat Callaghan down in the Chancellor's chair and placed before him a carefully prepared brief 2½ inches thick. It began with the stark and simple assessment that the Treasury anticipated a massive balance of payments deficit this year between £700,000,000 . . .

Next morning Wilson, Brown, and Callaghan met to discuss the crisis. They discussed the whole balance of payments situation and possible ways to remedy it, including a surcharge on imports. They also discussed the pruning of government spending on 'prestige projects' – that is to say, projects that could not be justified in terms of economic advantage. Leaving Wilson to complete his list of Ministers, Brown and Callaghan went off to draw up a set of emergency proposals to put before the Cabinet as a draft White Paper within the next few days.

Among the 'prestige projects' ripe for the axe were four aircraft – Concorde, the TSR–2, the P–1154 supersonic vertical take-off fighter, and the HS.681 tactical transport. As Brown and Callaghan well knew, to cancel the military planes would be to provoke a storm of anger from the Service and aerospace lobbies. But Concorde's cancellation would cause even greater problems, because of its repercussions on relations with France. For this reason, according to sources in Whitehall at the time, the draft White Paper meticulously avoided naming any project specifically. It said simply that Ministers would hold a strict review of all expenditure, particularly of prestige projects that 'strain the balance of payments'.

Had this formula been kept, it is likely that Concorde would have gone to the scrap-heap along with the three military planes. (The P–1154 and HS.681 were cancelled three months later, and the TSR–2 five months later in April 1965.) But it was not. Between the Cabinet's discussion of the draft on Wednesday and the White Paper's presentation to Parliament the following Monday, the passage about 'prestige projects' was made stronger and more explicit. The reason for this change, it has been suggested, was political pressure from Washington.

Ever since Britain and France had moved towards supersonic cooperation in 1961 the Americans had, in their various ways, been worried. Their plane-makers feared that Concorde would clean up the long-haul aviation market; the US Treasury foresaw that a rival American supersonic transport programme would devour federal funds. The Presidential go-ahead on the winning design was expected at the end of the year – unless, of course, Britain and France dropped the Concorde. There was thus a considerable American interest in getting Concorde stopped.

According to a former British Minister, 'there was hardly a month [in the last year of the Conservative Government] when pressure of one kind or another was not brought to bear on us from across the Atlantic'. Among those employed for this purpose was the Secretary of State, Dean Rusk. Early in 1963 Rusk came to London to discuss the Vietnam war situation with Foreign Secretary, Sir Alec Douglas Home. At the end of his talks he surprised the Foreign Office by announcing that he also wished to speak with Julian Amery, the Minister of Aviation. To Amery he then put the delicate suggestion that the United States might find it easier to help Britain over her balance of payments difficulties if Britain dropped extravagant projects such as Concorde, that challenged a politically sensitive sector of the US economy or, like TSR–2, duplicated US military developments.

This American attitude had in no way changed when, in the third week of October 1964, the head of the new DEA, Sir Eric Roll, was sent to Washington with the advance draft of George Brown's White Paper then before the Cabinet. The Americans were visibly pleased with it, but said they had one reservation: Was it not possible to include an allusion to a *specific* economy in the aerospace sector?

Roll relayed this request to London, with the result that George Brown inserted an electrifying sentence into the White Paper. The Government, it said, *had already told the French that it specially wished to re-examine the Concorde project*.

These words were to be read on the morning the White Paper was presented to Parliament; there was still a weekend in which to inform Paris. Even so the shortness of the warning was bound to seem brusque. It was therefore decided that publication of the White Paper should be followed by an announcement that the Minister of Aviation, Roy Jenkins, was going to Paris to discuss a 're-examination' of Concorde with his French counterpart. He could then explain the urgency of the Government's reasons.

The position of Jenkins was somewhat anomalous. He was not a member of the Cabinet and had not been invited to serve in the Government until four days after the election, by which time Brown and Callaghan had been working on the White Paper for 72 hours. He was given no word of their intentions on Concorde, and it was not until four days later that he learned in a roundabout way what was planned. The information came from the Permanent Under-Secretary at the Ministry of Aviation, Sir Richard Way.

On Friday 23 October, three days before the White Paper was due to be published, Way was called to the Treasury by Sir William Armstrong and told that the Government intended to 're-negotiate' the Concorde agreement. He naturally supposed that Jenkins had also been told, by Brown or Callaghan, but could not be sure. He and Jenkins lunched the same day at Brook's Club, of which they were both members. Over the meal Way mentioned his talk with Armstrong. He found it was the first Jenkins knew of the matter.

The French, of course, were in the dark too, though four days after the election there had been British press reports, probably inspired by DEA, that Concorde might be reviewed at 'an early date'. The first word about Concorde to reach Paris – and then only the British Embassy – was on Saturday morning. It arrived after the Ambassador, Sir Pierson Dixon, had left for the country with (rather embarrassingly) Julian Amery, who until eight days before had been Minister of Aviation. While still in office, Amery had been invited for a weekend's shooting by Maurice Heurteux, chairman of the Hispano-Suiza aircraft engineering firm. After the election he telegraphed to Heurteux to make his excuses, but Heurteux had pressed him to keep the date as a friend.

The Foreign Office message reached the Embassy about ten o'clock. It said that in the present economic situation the Government had serious reservations about Concorde, and asked Pierson Dixon to inform the French Government at once. The message was taken by the Embassy duty officer, who promptly drove off into the country to track down the Ambassador in the middle of the Heurteux shoot. Dixon raced back to Paris and spent the evening trying to reach the French Foreign Minister, M. Couve de Murville. When he finally got through he was told that Couve was unable to speak to anyone until the next afternoon.

Dixon spent part of Sunday shooting – this time with the textile magnate, André Boussac – but came back to Paris early for another attempt to see a member of the French Government. He was still unable to reach Couve de Murville, but later managed to speak with another French Minister who said he was 'not greatly surprised' by the news.

Shortly after eight o'clock next morning the Ambassador succeeded in seeing Couve de Murville at the Quai d'Orsay and delivered the Foreign Office message. Then he went back to the

Embassy where Amery, who had spent the weekend as his house guest, was still in bed. He explained that within a few hours the French Press would be in full cry and that it might be embarrassing if they found the former Minister of Aviation at the Ambassador's residence. Amery was quick to see the point.

In London the White Paper was laid before the House of Commons at 11 a.m. It included the reference to re-examining Concorde and was followed by the announcement that Jenkins would be going to Paris 'shortly' for talks with the French. As news of the announcement reached the Ministry of Aviation in Whitehall, civil servants concerned with the Concorde project visited neighbouring offices giving the thumbs-down sign. 'We had no doubt', said one of them long afterwards, 'that for all the soft talk about a "review" of the project, this was the end.'

In Paris the Press had an anti-British field-day. There were also rumblings from the Elysée which next day caused the Ambassador to send London a storm warning. Jenkins had meanwhile been told to go to Paris on Wednesday morning. As he boarded his plane at Heathrow he was handed a message from the Foreign Office. He was likely to be received, it said, with 'cold enmity'.

Jenkins arrived in Paris with an impossible mission. The Anglo–French agreement, a treaty in all but name, contained no mechanism for unilateral withdrawal. In addition the French had been antagonized by the shortness of the warning. The British delegation, consisting of Jenkins, Richard Way, and Morien Morgan, was met at Orly and taken to the Embassy, where it co-opted Tony Holden, the Civil Air attaché, to act as interpreter. (Jenkins spoke elegant French but did not trust his knowledge of technical terms.) The meeting with the Transport Minister, Marc Jacquet, had been fixed for the afternoon. Dixon could not go because of another appointment, but entertained the delegation to lunch. One of those present observed that the Ambassador was 'obviously disconcerted' by the way the Labour Government had handled matters – an attitude that appeared to pervade the entire Foreign Office.

The French received Jenkins with cool courtesy. Jacquet was accompanied by a senior civil servant from the Ministry of Transport and another from the Ministry of Technology, the two Ministries jointly responsible for the Concorde programme. All three Frenchmen were hearing the British position for the first time. When Jenkins had finished, Jacquet said his Government would wish to discuss the proposals and would reply as soon as possible. The meeting lasted less than an hour. Next day Jenkins met the Defence Minister, Pierre Messmer, to discuss the continuation of various Anglo–French military projects, and flew home.

The French reaction took a while to develop. Jenkins could have had no indication of it when, on the evening of his return, he invited the air correspondent of the *Sunday Times*, Ian Coulter, and myself, the air correspondent of the *Observer*, to his office at the Ministry of Aviation. His Chief Information Officer, Donald Grant, was also present. It was at the end of a long day and he poured out four large gins before attempting to explain the subtlety of the Government's position. He said the Government had every hope that the French would agree to a 're-assessment' of Concorde. By this he made it clear that he meant cancellation, on which he said a decision could not be long delayed. Weighing his remarks afterwards, both Coulter and I decided that the Government intended to announce cancellation before Parliament rose for the Christmas recess. On the following Sunday 1 November, both our stories used the phrase 'dead duck by Christmas' – a coincidence which made it seem, wrongly, that these words had been used by the Minister himself.

In fact, before our stories appeared, the obstacles to a quick cancellation were becoming clear. On Friday, the day after talking to us, Jenkins visited the Foreign Office, where he spoke with the Foreign Secretary, Patrick Gordon Walker. During this talk he learned for the first time of the legal complications of the Anglo–French agreement. He also realized that the Foreign Office, alerted by Pierson Dixon, had become gravely alarmed at the effect of a unilateral withdrawal on Anglo–French relations and was doing everything possible to prevent it. It was Patrick Gordon Walker who now pressed the Cabinet to take the advice of the Government's Law Officers before committing the country to an embarrassing and irreversible course. This it agreed to do; with the result that when, on

Monday, the French Press picked up the British Sunday newspaper stories, Whitehall was ready to deny that the Government had proposed anything as drastic as cancellation.

On 6 November *The Times* said the Government had still not taken a decision on Concorde. On 10 November the French denied reports (which they were suspected of having put out themselves) that they had asked the Soviet Union to take Britain's place in the project.* Finally on 13 November the French Government replied to the British proposals.

It was ready, it said primly, to review the Concorde 'at any time'; but it saw no reason to review it at that particular moment. It also recalled that the Anglo–French agreement, at Britain's request, contained no provision for either side to withdraw without the other's consent. It further reminded Britain that the agreement had been registered at the Hague Court.

The French reply was put before the Cabinet, which submitted it to the Attorney-General, Sir Elwyn Jones. Two days later he gave his opinion: if Britain pulled out, France would have a case against her in international law and could, if she wished, sue for nearly £200 million damages – more than the estimated cost of completing Britain's share of the programme.

The fate of Concorde now hung in the balance while the Cabinet wrestled with the overall economic crisis. Several Ministers, including Gordon Walker and, from 23 January, his successor, Michael Stewart, wanted all attempts at withdrawal to be abandoned. Others, like Denis Healey, accepted the Attorney-General's legal interpretation but doubted that the French, for political reasons, would actually go to law.

Callaghan and Brown were drifting into opposite camps. Callaghan would still have liked to cancel, but Brown, a committed 'European', was coming to realize that a protracted row over Concorde would wreck Labour's chances of getting Britain into Europe at a second attempt.

A powerful influence was exerted by the trade unions. At the beginning of November BAC's managing director, Sir George Edwards, had told the Government that cancellation would

* The reports were based on the fact the Soviet Foreign Trade Minister, Mr Patolichev, was in Paris to sign a Franco–Soviet trade agreement. A few weeks later, approaches were made to Sweden, Germany, Holland, and Belgium under a so-called 'European plan' to replace British participation.

oblige the Corporation to close down its Filton factory, causing extensive unemployment in Bristol and the South-West. As the crisis dragged on and work approached a standstill, workers at Filton and Toulouse saw their jobs disappearing and called on their trade unions to protect them. Eugène Montel, a veteran socialist and a deputy for Toulouse, flew to London to ginger up trade unionists in the Labour Party. From Britain Clive Jenkins, leader of the white-collar Association of Supervisory Staff, Executives and Technicians (ASSET), flew twice to Paris to plead for a compromise that would save Concorde by cutting its costs. The trade unions had meanwhile made at least one ministerial convert – the former trade-union leader Frank Cousins who, as Minister of Technology, shared responsibility for Concorde with Roy Jenkins.

Matters were allowed to drift until mid December when Britain came up with a compromise proposal: work on development would continue, but the programme should be limited to the construction of two prototypes. This would mean dropping the building of two 'pre-production' aircraft and the setting up of a production line. It was also proposed to call off, temporarily, the advanced development programme for bringing the plane up to airline standards. The revised scheme would have cost each country only £100 million but would have delayed the in-service date by at least two years. The French refused even to consider it.

At the beginning of January the Government tried another tactic, when it sought to construe the 1962 Agreement as being merely to *develop* the supersonic transport, leaving *production* to be governed by separate agreement. When the French rejected this also, it was faced with the true situation: either it pulled out and accepted the risk of legal action; or it went ahead, ate humble pie, and, by making a show of enthusiasm for Concorde, tried to salvage what it could of its relations with Paris. Almost alone, Denis Healey stuck out for cancellation. The rest of the Cabinet decided to call it a day. The deciding factor, one of them admitted later, was not the amount of damages that Britain might have to pay, but the stigma of being hauled before the International Court.

On 18 January the Cabinet finally decided to capitulate, and

Jenkins was again ordered to fly to Paris. This time, however, he left in secrecy, in an executive jet lent by the Hawker Siddeley company, and no one in the Press was aware of his trip until three weeks later.

Two days after delivering the message of surrender to Jacquet, Jenkins told the House of Commons: 'We have now completed the review of the Concorde project which we set in hand in October, and we have exchanged views with the French Government. We had, and we still retain, some doubts about the financial and economic aspects of the project. We have, however, been much impressed by the confidence of our French partners, and the Prime Minister has informed the French Prime Minister that we stand by the treaty obligations into which the last Government decided to enter.'

Hansard records that there were Opposition interruptions and cries of 'Oh' as Jenkins went on to say: 'Now that the uncertainty over the future of the project has been removed, I am sure that all those concerned with it on both sides of the Channel will press forward with a real sense of purpose. In this they will have the full backing of Her Majesty's Government.'

5. Rationalizing Surrender

Recalling the Concorde's 'cancellation' crisis six years later, Harold Wilson was to describe how his Government had found the French

unwilling to cancel or even to review the project. What is more, the Concorde arrangement was not a commercial agreement which could have allowed the two parties to break off the programme when costs escalated or commercial prospects grew dim. It was the subject of an international treaty, registered at the United Nations and subject to all the procedures of the International Court at the Hague. Had we unilaterally denounced the treaty, we were told, we could have been taken to the International Court, where there would have been little doubt that it would have found against us. This would have meant that the French could then have gone ahead with the project no matter what the cost, giving us no benefit either from the research or the ultimate product. But the Court would almost certainly have ruled that we should be mulcted for half the cost. At that time half the cost was estimated . . . at £190 millions. This we should have had to pay, with nothing to show for it, the result of what we considered an improvident treaty on the part of Julian Amery . . . Faced with this situation, we had little alternative but to go on.*

Had we? Shortly after the British admission of defeat a senior French Minister told his British opposite number that if only the British Government had persisted in its efforts for a week or two longer, the French would have given in. He said there was extreme disquiet about Concorde in the French Treasury, and indeed on the part of many people in the French aviation industry who were now much wiser about the plane's economic problems. These included the head of Sud Aviation, M. Hereil and

* *The Labour Government 1964-70: A Personal Record*, Harold Wilson, Weidenfeld & Nicholson and Michael Joseph, 1971, pp. 61-2.

his deputy, General Ziegler. (Hereil resigned shortly afterwards because of his grave reservations, but Ziegler took his place and became a tireless enthusiast.)

In London doubts about the Cabinet's interpretation of the Law Officers' advice continued to fester. Roy Jenkins, caught in the mill of Anglo–French frictions, respected the Attorney-General's *legal* judgment. Even so, he doubted whether the Cabinet had been right to give in. After all, the Law Officers had merely been asked how Britain would stand in law if she pulled out. They had not been asked to say (nor could they have done so) what action the French Government was actually likely to take in such a case. The Attorney-General had made this clear when he submitted his opinion.

Jenkins later regretted not having pressed this point. But after the initial approach to the French had gone wrong, it seemed too late to reverse matters. The Government was then on the verge of cancelling £1,200 million worth of military projects – the P–1154, the HS.681, and the TSR–2 – and there was a limit to what Ministers were ready to take in the way of outraged protests from the trade unions. It was also a fact that he was a relatively junior Minister, not in the Cabinet, and thus without much influence.

How had the Government so miscalculated the situation? The question is all the more puzzling in that only a few months earlier the binding nature of the Anglo–French agreement had been noted by the House of Commons Estimates Committee. It had also been freely discussed in Whitehall. The agreement itself could be read in two minutes.

The kindest explanation could be simply the haste with which new Ministers had to master their jobs in the midst of an economic crisis. In the case of DEA the Department itself was new. Born of a talk between Brown and Wilson in a taxi one night, it had not even been assembled when Brown composed the White Paper. And Sir Eric Roll, whom Brown chose as its permanent head, was an expert not in European matters, but in economic liaison with Washington where, until a few weeks before, he had been the chief Treasury representative. Had DEA been properly established, Brown might have known more about the strength of French feeling towards Concorde.

He might also have acted less precipitately if there had been better liaison between other departments.

In his book* Brown makes no secret of the frictions arising between DEA and the Treasury, which felt that the former was trespassing on its territory. In the case of Concorde there seems to have been an equally disastrous gap in DEA's communications with the Foreign Office and the Ministry of Aviation.

At the Ministry of Aviation senior civil servants were certainly well aware of the binding nature of the 1962 agreement. One of them – a scientist – recalled later: 'The scientists were more pro-Concorde than the administrative heads. We were never really worried about the Labour Government's threat to withdraw. We knew that the French had the power of veto. We simply went on with the job.' Another put it more bluntly: 'It was George Brown who saved Concorde, by naming it the "Brown Paper". But for that the French would have been glad to get out of it. It was almost as if he wanted to offend the one body – the French Government – whose cooperation we needed for cancellation.'

Early in February, the Government announced cancellation of the P–1154 and the HS.681. The protests from the Service and industrial lobbies were less violent than had been expected, perhaps because the planes were still in the design stage. There was also much doubt about their military necessity.† But the big row – over TSR–2 – was still to come.

TSR–2 (the initials stood for Tactical Reconnaissance and Strike) had been begun in 1959 as a replacement for Canberra medium bomber. It was supposed to cost £90 million, but by the 1964 election campaign the official estimate had already risen to £200–250 million and was expected to rise much higher still. These figures reflected its complexity. Its *forte* was its ability to fly supersonically below the arc of enemy radar defences with

---

* *In My Way,* George Brown, Gollancz, 1971, Penguin, 1972.

† The P–1154 had already been rejected by the Royal Navy, which preferred th fixed-wing American Phantom. Following the cancellation of the P–1154, the Phantom became the new ground-attack fighter for the RAF also. Instead of the four-jet HS.681 the RAF was given the American turbo-propellor C–130 Hercules. The cost of these American planes was £236 million, less than a third of the cost of the British originals.

the aid of terrain-following radar. It could transmit television pictures of a battlefield to a commander several hundreds of miles away, or launch a nuclear or conventional bomb with unprecedented accuracy. On its performance specification it justified the claim that it was the most advanced aircraft in the world. But could Britain afford it?

The answer unanimously given by the Cabinet was No. But in February 1965 Wilson wanted a breathing space. Defensively he let it be understood that TSR–2 was to be given a six months' reprieve – and at the BAC factory at Warton, Lancashire, work was hurried forward in the belief that, if only the TSR–2 could amass enough flying hours, the outcry against cancellation would be overwhelming.

The first of seven prototypes had flown on 28 September, the pilot, Roland Beamont, having volunteered to take off from Warton in full knowledge that the plane's Olympus engines had four times exploded on the test-bed, and that the fault, though diagnosed, was still uncorrected. In the next six months Beamont continued the programme from the Aeroplane and Armament Experimental Establishment at Boscombe Down in Wiltshire. It was a gallant effort but did not alter the fact that TSR–2 was in the same class as Concorde – a highly advanced technological project, which Britain did not need and could certainly not afford.

On 5 April the axe fell. Cancellation was announced by Callaghan in his budget speech. This was followed by a statement from Healey explaining that, with the approval of the Air Staff, TSR–2 would be replaced in the RAF inventory by the American F–111*.

So violent was the reaction of the Opposition, and so determined the Government that TSR–2 should be beyond possibility of resurrection, that orders were given to break up the finished and half-finished prototypes where they stood. No event in British aviation had ever caused so much feeling.

The cancellation of TSR–2 was the corollary of Concorde's reprieve. The death of the one and the reprieve of the other were rationalized eight months later by the report of the Select Committee under Sir Edmund Plowden, which had been asked

* The order for 50 F–111s was later cancelled in the 1967 devaluation crisis.

to examine the problems of the aircraft industry. The committee said that Britain should never again attempt the largest and most complex types of military aircraft. On other major projects, both civil and military, it recommended 'wholehearted cooperation' with European countries, aimed at evolving a 'European industry'. It further declared that the industry had no 'predestined place' in the economy and must adapt itself to a reduced level of government support.

Though many of the Plowden proposals came to be disregarded in the end they supplied a philosophy on which to go forward again. But in prescribing the form of this collaboration Plowden drew attention to the basic weakness of the Concorde programme.

In ... Concorde there has been a broad split of work on each of the three main elements of the programme, airframe, engines and equipment. A division of this kind entails penalties. There are problems of devising a split which is both technically workable and politically acceptable. And the resulting programme may well be difficult to manage and fall short of the cheapest and most efficient way of doing the job.

On 18 February a junior Minister, Austin Albu, had told the House of Commons that, although the Government intended to press ahead 'energetically' with Concorde, it also intended 'to examine its economic potential from time to time and not to continue with an open-ended commitment'. The hollowness of this promise soon became evident.

In March the programme began to fall behind schedule. The first flight date, originally intended to be in 1966, was put off until 'early 1968'. Costs had already gone up to £250 million because of the previous year's decision to increase the seating capacity. Orders had been better than might have been expected, considering that airlines were still paying heavily for the first generation of subsonic jets; but the trouble with these 'orders', which now totalled 45, was that they were not orders in the accepted sense but merely 'options'. In return for a small deposit they gave the option-holder a guaranteed delivery position. This was without risk because, if the programme fell through or the plane failed to perform as the option contract specified, the deposit was returnable. The taking of the option generally attracted a fair amount of publicity – more, perhaps, than the customer could have obtained for the same sum spent on advertising.

The first 12 'options' had not been even of this order, but merely reservations made by the British and French Governments on behalf of BOAC and Air France. The state airlines paid no deposits for these planes – and all other customers were entitled to the return of their deposits if BOAC and Air France failed to place firm orders later on.

The first real options had been taken out in the summer of 1963 after presentations to overseas airlines. On 4 June Pan-American Airways (which had meanwhile reserved delivery positions for the American Supersonic Transport) signed a contract for six. Another American airline, Continental, took six in July, American Airlines four in October, and Trans-World Airlines four in November. In September Middle East Airlines took two options. Next April the Australian airline QANTAS took four. In the meantime BOAC, Air France, and Pan-American each increased their options to eight. These increases were due to the 1963–4 capacity increase. Those by BOAC and Air France were accompanied by a statement that the state airlines were now going to put down deposits like everyone else.

Such was the 'order' position in 1964 when the makers were telling their Governments that they foresaw sales of 300–400 Concordes even in competition with an American SST.

But after the QANTAS 'order' in April the build-up faltered. The reason became clear the following month during a discussion by the Technical Committee of the International Air Transport Association in Beirut. The new 118-seat capacity was still too small in view of what was now known about supersonic operating costs.

Once again it was necessary to embark on a major re-design; and again this was opposed by Sud Aviation, which simply wanted to get the prototype flying. After much argument the matter was settled by British and French officials on the Concorde Directing Committee telling the companies that the design must be revised.

The new configuration, bringing the capacity to 136 seats

(and again adding greatly to the costs) was evolved throughout the autumn and winter of the Anglo–French 'cancellation' row. It mainly involved changing the curl and camber of the wing tips. This gave greater lift without increasing the wingspan and supersonic drag. To avoid delaying the first flight, the change was to be made to the two 'pre-production' aircraft* but not to the two prototypes whose design had been frozen six months before. The changes were announced to customers in May 1965 and increased the weight of the aircraft to about 350,000lb.

In the following weeks BAC and Sud Aviation made efforts to sell Concorde to European airlines, which had so far shown great coolness. As part of the campaign it was suggested that European countries might share in production work with a view to founding a 'European' aircraft industry. Whether it would have been possible to bring in new partners at this stage is doubtful, though there was still scope for farming some work on sub-contract. In the event the Italians were not interested, Alitalia being committed to the longer-range American SST; and Germany, after making sounds of encouragement, knocked the scheme on the head when Chancellor Erhard said the project had progressed too far for the Federal Republic to participate. (What the Germans *were* interested in, it transpired, was a European airbus, on which Jenkins and Jacquet had begun talks in February.)

Talks with other overseas airlines were more successful. In September Japan Air Lines took out options on three Concordes, saying that the new design made it possible to fly the commercially important Tokyo–Honolulu route. Sabena followed with two options in November; Eastern with two in May 1966 (which they later increased to four, and finally six a year later); Braniff with three; United Airlines with six; and Air Canada with four in December 1966.

Finally Lufthansa – previously a non-customer because Concorde had lacked the necessary range to fly Frankfurt–New York – acquired three options in March 1967.

This brought the total of options on Concorde to 74, and the number of customer airlines to 16. And there the figure stuck

---

* These were to be as close as possible to the production model to permit their use for airworthiness certification. There was a difference in length of 11 feet.

– less than a quarter of the way to the makers' sales target and well short of the 129 orders that had by now been placed for the American SST.

The main reason for the standstill was Concorde's limited range and payload capacity. But another major reason, which the makers would have given almost anything to remove, was the growing conviction of airlines that they would not be allowed to operate supersonically over inhabited land areas because of the sonic bang.

6. Bangs and Super-Bangs

It was the revelation of the 'boom' problem that first alerted most people to the fact that the supersonic transport posed a threat to the quality of everyday life. It was thus in the tradition of a whole succession of twentieth-century technological innovations, beginning with the internal combustion engine and embracing its consequences, the motorway and airport, by which the existence of the many was regularly degraded for the benefit of a privileged minority.

With the supersonic transport the benefit to the few was little more than a convenience – a few hours' time-saving two or three times a year in the case of most users. The penalty, on the other hand, would be harsh and universal if the supersonic

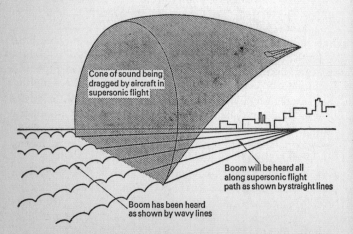

Cone of sound being dragged by aircraft in supersonic flight

Boom will be heard all along supersonic flight path as shown by straight lines

Boom has been heard as shown by wavy lines

Figure 4. The Sonic boom.

aircraft became the accepted form of travel that the makers intended.

The sonic boom (or bang) of an aircraft is like the bow wave of a ship. Just as a ship sets up a bow wave throughout its voyage, a supersonic aircraft creates a sonic bang during the entire supersonic sector of its flight, although people in the path of the boom experience it only once – at the moment it passes over them. What they feel is a sudden increase in air pressure which is the shock wave caused by the unreadiness of air to part for any object moving faster than sound (the phenomenon described in Chapter 1).

The intensity of the bang is expressed as 'overpressure', i.e. the increase of pressure over the normal atmospheric pressure, measured in psi (pounds per square inch). With a supersonic airliner having the weight and dimensions of Concorde the overpressure created by the shock wave is generally between 1 and 1.5 psi; but because the shock wave rebounds from the ground the overpressure is always doubled.*

This might seem a small increase – no more than the pressure increase caused by the downward plunge of an express lift. But the capacity of the bang to shock and do damage is due to the speed with which it occurs – the change of pressure takes place within one thousandth of a second. Another factor determining the damage potential is the *duration* of the overpressure. This varies with the size of the aircraft. The bang caused by a supersonic airliner is likely to be much more serious than that of a supersonic fighter.

Though there is plenty of evidence, e.g. from Oklahoma tests (see p. 62), to suggest that even 'nominal' bangs of 2–3 psi can never be acceptable, the main objection to supersonic flying over populated areas is the occurrence of 'freak' bangs having up to four times the intensity of nominal bangs.

These 'super-bangs' can be caused by a variety of factors. One is atmospheric focusing due to differing temperatures and wind velocities. Another is the aircraft's transition from subsonic to supersonic flight, which causes shock waves from successive flight sectors to reach the same place on the ground

* This 'doubling' should not be confused with the double bang caused by separate shock-waves from the front and tail of large supersonic aircraft.

simultaneously. Yet another cause is the reflection effect when a shock wave hits a hard surface such as a city street or building and bounces back. A fourth is manoeuvres at supersonic

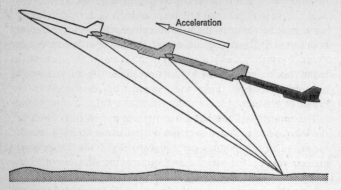

Figure 5. As speed increases the angle of the shock wave becomes more acute. This causes a 'focusing effect' when the aircraft accelerates.

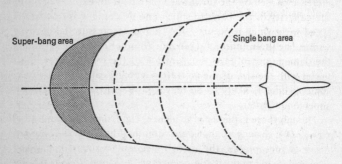

Figure 6. Ground pattern of super-bangs created by acceleration.

speed which cause the bang to occur with varying force in different directions. A super-bang due to any of these things – or a combination of them – can appear very capricious, causing one house or street to be extensively damaged, while neighbouring streets or houses escape entirely.

The causes of bangs and super-bangs were well known long

before Concorde was even thought of. In 1953 the Minister of Supply had warned Parliament that there was no sign of a solution for the problem of bangs from military aircraft. 'We are probably in for some rather noisy times,' he told MPs cheerfully. Three days later *The Times* published a letter from a senior lecturer at the College of Aeronautics, Cranfield, saying that supersonic flying could be permitted only over the sea or at great heights, since the danger of an enemy 'or even a thoughtless friend' raising the roof merely by flying past was a real one.

Seven years later the airlines and public were warned about the problem of the boom and the dangers of a 'supersonic race' by Bo Lundberg's article in the *New Scientist*. Lundberg wrote:

Primarily for medical and social reasons, supersonic aviation – be it in day or night time, over sea or over sparsely populated areas – should be permitted only if the operators can guarantee that the sonic booms will be below a specified limit – a limit set so low that light sleepers will normally not be awakened by sonic bangs of that magnitude. At the present state of the art, and in the foreseeable future, such a requirement cannot be satisfied economically, for it would limit size of supersonic aircraft to fighter-like dimensions.*

Yet in spite of such warnings, which certainly caused discussion in the Society of British Aircraft Constructors, pressure from the industry for the supersonic project continued undiminished, and anyone who questioned its wisdom was regarded as a reactionary or a crank. That the 'cranks' finally became the voice of the majority was due to the efforts of a number of environment groups, whose growth and influence was a major phenomenon of the 1960s. In Britain the long-established Noise Abatement Society had been fighting all forms of noise pollution since 1959. With the coming of the jets it was joined in its battle against aircraft noise by a number of very vigorous local associations, mostly in the neighbourhood of airports. These became federated in two large national groups – the British Association for the Control of Aircraft Noise (BACAN) and the UK Federation Against Aircraft Nuisance – both of which kept a close watch on Concorde's ground noise, the Federation in particular making effective use of scientific

* The *New Scientist*, Feb. 1961.

equipment to monitor take-offs and landings by the Concorde prototype.

But the organization whose efforts to stop Concorde overshadowed all others was the Anti-Concorde Project.

Its founder was a teacher of handicapped children, Richard Wiggs, who came from a family of Hertfordshire Quakers. In the mid 1960s he had become active in a campaign to secure for leaseholders in his home town of Letchworth the benefits of the new Leasehold Reform Act, which a powerful landlord, the Letchworth Garden City Corporation, was seeking to have modified in Parliament. It was a David and Goliath situation in which Wiggs used many of the techniques which he later applied against the Supersonic Transport – letters to newspapers, telephone calls to editors, the buying of advertising space to put the leaseholders' case before the public. In the end the 'Letchworth Amendment' was defeated and Wiggs could concentrate on a bigger matter.

'I called it the Anti-Concorde Project, rather than Anti-Concorde Campaign,' he explains, 'because "campaign" had a rather defeatist ring about it. I was thinking of the Campaign for Nuclear Disarmament, which I'd also supported, but which hadn't got very far.'

The idea crystallized after the Labour Government failed to go through with its intention to cancel Concorde in 1964–5. Wiggs says he was already deeply worried about the effects of the sonic boom, and felt that if only the Government had been able to call on the support of a lobby of 'civilized people' to counterbalance the aerospace lobby it might have stuck to its guns. His moment of decision came in September 1966 when the *Observer* published a letter from a reader, D. W. Rowell, who said he would be ready to support an anti-Concorde movement if only somebody would organize it.

Wiggs wrote to the *Observer* offering to get a movement going, and received about 80 replies. A second letter to the paper, announcing the Project's inauguration, brought another 80 replies, and Wiggs started operations by sending out duplicated letters to all who had written to him – the first of a stream of letters that has poured from his duplicating machine ever since.

'I intended,' he says, 'to form a committee and take a back seat. I knew nothing about noise, and not much about aeroplanes.' But things worked out differently. Finding, after his first two letters to the *Observer*, that he could get no more letters into the Press, he decided to buy advertising space. In July 1967 he placed column-length advertisements in the *New Scientist*, *New Society*, and the *New Statesman*. The advertisements brought 'thousands' of replies, including letters from such valuable adherents as Lady Snow and Sir Alec Guinness.*

Wiggs now gave up part-time teaching to answer correspondence and took a whole summer holiday, with the help of his family and student labour, to deal with it. One of his ideas at this stage was that 500 supporters should pledge 0.3 per cent of their income to keep the Project going. A number responded; but the main response came in *ad hoc* gifts which have since continued to provide the organization's main income (in 1972 about £7,000 a year). Wiggs takes a £2,500 salary for his full-time organizational work which, to judge from his unceasing correspondence with newspaper editors and air correspondents, he fully earns.

The American counterpart of the Anti-Concorde Project, the Citizens' League Against the Sonic Boom, appeared on the scene about five months later, in March 1967. Its founders were two highly respected New Englanders: Dr William Shurcliff, a Senior Research Associate at the Cambridge Electron Accelerator project of Harvard University, who had been an assistant of Dr Vannevar Bush at the Office of Scientific Research and Development in the Second World War; and Professor John J. Edsall, another Harvard academic, with whom Richard Wiggs had started correspondence after publishing his first *New Scientist* advertisement.

The League adopted the same propaganda techniques as the Project with astounding success. By 1970, when the SST was cancelled, it had acquired many thousands of supporters. It also forged links with other American pressure groups such as the Environmental Defence Fund and the Sierra Club, which were devoted to conservation of the environment on a wider

* The Concorde split the Theatre as it split opinion elsewhere. In 1971 Sir Laurence Olivier declared himself wholly in favour of the plane.

front. Another powerful body organizing popular resistance to the SST and Concorde was the international Friends of the Earth.

In one respect the American movement enjoyed an advantage over Wiggs's campaign. The American political system provided greater opportunities than the British for forcing the Administration to publish awkward facts; and it was in the tradition of this more open system that the US Government empowered the Federal Aviation Agency to hold the world's first (and only) series of tests to check public reaction to the creation of sonic bangs over cities.

The first sonic boom tests were held over St Louis, Missouri in 1961–2. They subjected the city of 750,000 people to 150 supersonic overflights and produced 5,000 individual complaints. In 1964 a smaller series of tests was made over Chicago (pop. 3,500,000), Milwaukee (pop. 741,000) and Pittsburgh (pop. 604,000). In 1967, 365 flights were made over the 45,000 people living near Edwards Air Force Base, California. But the largest and most carefully planned series was over Oklahoma City in 1964. This lasted five months, involved 1,254 flights, and directed the boom at 324,000 people.

Oklahoma was chosen for the tests because of its climatic conditions, which ranged from February frosts to the thundery heat of May. This made it possible to register 'super-bangs' caused by hot and humid air. It was also the site of a large Air Force base. The object of the tests was to discover how the citizens of an average town would react to booms occurring several times each day, seven days a week, and to ascertain the maximum overpressure to which people could be subjected. The flights were made by B–58 bombers, whose pilots were ordered to fly at altitudes between 36,000 and 44,000 feet, where the B–58 created booms as intense as those expected from the much larger Supersonic Transport at 60,000 to 80,000 feet. The overpressures were intended to be in the 1–2 psi range.

The flights, at 1,200 m.p.h., took place four times a day, between 7 a.m. and 1.20 p.m. The first flight, which always took place at 7 o'clock, created a bang sufficiently loud for thousands of people to use it as an alarm clock. A typical description was 'rather like a cannon'. But in cloudy weather the bangs were much sharper. Some motorists reported that the shock jerked their hands from the steering wheel. The booms broke windows, cracked plaster, warped window panes, shifted walls. One of the first damage claims was for the cracking of a swimming pool in a $90,000 luxury home. An office building had 135 windows shattered. But the worst damage was done in the ramshackle homes of Oklahoma's negro quarter, where several people narrowly escaped serious injury from falling ceilings.

In July the Federal Aviation Administrator, Mr Najeeb Halaby, had to admit that the booms had caused more serious problems than the FAA had bargained for. Although the maximum overpressure planned had been 2 psi, often more than 3 psi had been experienced. One of the earliest consequences was an increase in nervous complaints reported by the health authorities – though this did not dampen the hope of the city's Commerce Department that Oklahoma might eventually become the supersonic airport of Mid America. By the end of the series in June 15,000 complaints had been filed. Six years later litigation, which was still proceeding, had resulted in the award of $218,647 in compensation, the largest payment being of $10,000 for damage to a new house. Other payments were for cracked tiles, fallen plaster, and the breakage of crockery falling from shelves.

One result of the Oklahoma tests was that when, a year later, the Federal Government awarded design contracts for a supersonic transport, it stipulated that the plane should be capable of economic operation even if prevented from flying supersonically over populated areas. Another result was the arming of the SST's opponents with a large quantity of statistics on which to fight the project, some of which could be used by their friends overseas.

The United States Government, though it was to commit gross mistakes in its supersonic programme, at least acted logically in holding the FAA boom tests before commissioning the design of the SST. The British and French Governments held no tests and imposed no conditions as to operating profitability. Later the makers of the Concorde were to insist that it would command an adequate market even if there were to be a ban on supersonic flying over land. But in 1965 there was strong suspicion that they had 'sold' Concorde to their governments by concealing the fact that a ban would halve its sales. That the Conservative Government, which favoured the Concorde for political reasons, had not inquired too deeply into the boom problem was understandable. What was more puzzling was the refusal of the Labour Government to conduct proper tests.

Shortly after Labour took office, senior civil servants at the Ministry of Aviation proposed a series of tests over a typical British city. The city selected was Hull. For months, in great secrecy, the proposal was tossed between Departments – finally to be turned down on the grounds that there would be an outcry from the 'guinea pig' area. After this timid decision the Government was obliged to base its crucial evaluation of the boom problem in Europe on the borrowed results of the American tests at Oklahoma.

In April 1965 a curious exercise, evidently intended to allay public disquiet, was held at an RAF airfield in Huntingdonshire. The Minister of Aviation, Roy Jenkins, was present with a group of Pressmen, as a Lightning interceptor was flown across the airfield at three different heights, designed to produce bangs of 1, 1.5, and 2 psi. When the flights were over a technician exploded, without warning, a stick of gelignite, apparently to show that the bang had been less disturbing. The demonstration, which produced no 'super-bangs', was followed by newspaper stories saying that the boom problem had been overplayed.

A more elaborate, but equally ineffectual, test of public reaction was held in the summer of 1967, when the Ministry of Technology, which since the previous year had been under Anthony Wedgwood Benn, MP for Bristol South-East, arranged for the RAF to stage timed flights over southern England. There were four over London, five over Bristol, and two over Dorset. Again the plane used was the Lightning which, because of its size and weight, produced a smaller bang than Concorde, though this was supposed to be offset by its altitude.

Unlike the Oklahoma tests, most of the 1967 flights were made without an announcement about the exact time and place. This caused some to go almost unnoticed in certain areas, and in general, where the boom was within normal limits, there

Monuments Inspectorate found damage at the priceless Romanesque church at Vezelay which necessitated the shoring up of three bays, and the sudden collapse of the tower at the castle of Genelon.

But *observed* cases of damage were only part of the picture. The crux of the matter was divined by the Principal Inspector, M. Parent, when he wrote in 1968:

How many buildings are being secretly damaged little by little? How many falls of material have simply not been noticed and how much invisible, but nevertheless *real*, damage is being done? Here are inextricably mixed the variable effects of the general ageing due to the natural instability of the soil, to the state of the materials, to other accidental shakings, and the daily effects of 'bangs' in particularly exposed regions . . . This state of things justifies our alarm, because one can conclude from it *statistically* that the bang diminishes the total duration and consequently the volume at any given date of our artistic heritage.*

* *Les Monuments Historiques de France, Janvier–Mars 1968.*

was no public outcry. But whenever the boom was int
by reflection or focusing – which happened frequentl
reaction was sharp. In the course of a week the Ministry
board was repeatedly jammed, and the small organizat
up to deal with complaints completely overwhelme
arrangements had been made to measure public reaction
organized poll (as had been done in Oklahoma). Nor
Ministry attempt to process scientifically the thousands o
plaints that got through to it. All that the 'tests' demon:
was that the Government had been over-optimistic
damage, which the Minister of State, John Stonehous
said would be negligible. As a result of the tests the G
ment had to pay out more than £4,000 in compensation, i
ing £1,000 to 146 victims of broken glass, £1,400 for 93 da
ceilings, and £300 for three cases of personal injury.

The defenders of Concorde and the American SS'
always said that there was no risk of damage to soundly
structed buildings from overpressures of the kind that mig
expected from supersonic airline operation (generally spe
by the Americans as about 2.4lb. per square inch). But wh:
'soundly constructed' mean? The callousness of the phras
demonstrated in 1967 when three people were killed in
South of France by a sonic boom from a military plane v
caused the collapse of a farmhouse. The damage to an
buildings in France – the only West European country w
military planes were regularly allowed to fly supersonically
the countryside – has been a national scandal. In 1964
Custodians of Historic Monuments could already cite 100
in 20 departments, chiefly in southern, south-western, and
tral France. The most serious and frequent damage was
bursting, breaking, and loosening of stained-glass windows.
worst cases were in the cathedral at Troyes, at Mozac, an
the Yonne Valley. But the bulging of windows was also ol
ved in the cathedrals at Strasbourg and at Le Mans. In 20
there had been damage to masonry, ranging from sudden cr
ing and a fall of material to the total collapse of a belfry to
In other cases there had been damage to roof coverings,
nishings, and decorations, especially plasterwork – inclu
damage to mural paintings at Oiron. Later the Hist

CF–5

7. Estimates and Guesstimates

Between 1962 and 1973 Concorde's sales prospects were variously estimated by the makers at between 160 and 500 aircraft. How such figures were reached was a mystery that regularly interested the House of Commons Committee on Estimates and Expenditure. The industry's phrase for the process was 'guesstimate'. In Concorde's case it generally meant projecting the current annual traffic increase over a period of years and dividing the total by the plane's productivity in terms of passenger-miles annually. Allowance was made (generously in favour of Concorde) for sharing the enlarged market with projected rivals. No allowance was made for fluctuations in the growth rate of air traffic, nor for major developments in subsonic design, which were to be a very unsettling factor indeed.

In 1962, according to BAC sources, the Cabinet had decided to finance the development of a supersonic airliner on the strength of estimates by BAC and Sud Aviation that each could sell 80 of their respective supersonic designs, the BAC-223 and the Super-Caravelle. The Americans, who were not yet in the supersonic business, were then talking of a supersonic market by the early 1980s of about 500. Two years later, when traffic growth pointed to an increase of about 15 per cent annually, BAC and Sud Aviation talked of selling 300–400 Concordes, and the Americans, backed by computer studies, of a total supersonic market of 1,400. But these improved forecasts ignored the possibility of a ban on supersonic overflying. When the latter was allowed for, Concorde sales estimates had to be reduced to 200–250, because many of the hoped-for sales were to operators of internal services in the United States.

The Anglo–French estimates presupposed that with a three-year lead Concorde could win between a quarter and a third of the supersonic market, and that, after the American SST came into service, it would remain in demand on less heavily used routes. But when the SST fell behind schedule and Concorde's lead lengthened, the BAC sales estimate went up again. Thus in 1966 BAC's Concorde sales manager, Pat Burgess, was telling British newspapers that *even with a total ban on overland supersonic overflying* and a 26 per cent supersonic fare surcharge, Concorde sales would reach 400 by 1980. In July the next year Sir George Edwards told the Aero Club of Washington that, with sales of 40–50 a year in the mid 1970s, the final figure could be about 500.

What these estimates most strangely ignored was a new and revolutionary development in air transport economics.

In April 1965 the Boeing Company, though deeply involved in the American SST programme, announced plans to build a giant *sub*sonic aircraft as a successor to the 707, of which it had sold more than 600. The new giant, to be called the 747, would be a civil adaptation of the military design with which Boeing had lost to Lockheed in the recent competition to supply a strategic transport for the US Air Force. Carrying 499 people* at ranges of up to 6,000 miles or more, Boeing's design hit the American air transport industry at a moment of unprecedented traffic expansion. It promised a reduction in direct operating costs of about 30 per cent.

Within a few weeks Pan-American, which had been the first airline to order the 707, signed an order for 25. Other airlines followed, many of them over-ordering under the makers' sales pressure and creating an avalanche. By 1967 the order book stood at 206, including orders by BOAC, Air France, and other customers for Concorde. Boeing's success inevitably attracted others into the wide-bodied jet market. Douglas announced the DC–10 and Lockheed the Tri-Star, both medium-haul planes capable of carrying upwards of 350 passengers.

The 'jumbos' were a blow to Concorde in several ways. With a price of about £10 million (£2 million less than the then quoted price of Concorde) they absorbed a large amount of airline capital; they also led operators into financial difficulties by creating excessive capacity, especially on the North Atlantic,

* The maximum number allowed by its Certificate of Airworthiness. Initially most airlines installed about 350 seats. In 1973 a 700-seat version was planned.

where in 1970 the airlines were flying the equivalent of 100 empty 707s every day. But the most serious impact on Concorde arose from the big planes' low operating costs. These put the Concorde, which had been designed with the 170-seat 707 in mind, into a position where it could hardly compete as an investment.

Passenger appeal was also important. For although the Concorde was supposed to halve flight times, one of its drawbacks, for aerodynamic reasons, was that passengers would have to sit in a cabin only 8 feet 7½ inches wide. Visitors to the Concorde mock-ups at Filton and Orly already felt a touch of claustrophobia when comparing them with existing jets, whose interior width was 11½ feet. In the 747, with a cabin width of 20 feet, passengers for the first time had an aeroplane in which they could move about during the flight. This applied particularly to first-class passengers (Concorde's potential users) who were offered facilities that even the designers of the luxury airships of the 1930s never dreamed of.

Finally, the low-cost 'jumbos' were expected to accelerate the downward trend of fares with the result that middle-class Englishmen would be able to take winter holidays in Florida, and Americans in Fiji and the South Pacific.

Such was the stuff of airline publicity in 1968, on the eve of the jumbos entering service. But within two years the airlines had other preoccupations. The steady growth of traffic that had marked the 1960s had suddenly levelled off, and for some airlines actually became a decline. By 1972 a majority of airlines were operating 'in the red'. One reason for the setback was the world-wide recession which caused a fall in business travel. The other, which hit many 'scheduled' airlines with options on Concorde, was the loss of traffic to the so-called 'supplementals' operating the charter market outside the fare-fixing system of the International Air Transport Association.

This was the inauspicious moment when Concorde reached the advanced stage of development at which option holders were supposed to convert their options into firm orders so that the plane could be put into production.

The original first flight date, announced in 1965 and permanently displayed on notice boards at the Filton and Toulouse factories, had been 28 February 1968. This was for the French-assembled prototype, No. 001. According to the programme, the British-assembled prototype, 002, was to have flown in the following September. The two pre-production aircraft, 01 (British) and 02 (French) were to have flown on 31 December 1969 and 28 February 1970. The first three production aircraft, Nos. 1, 2, and 3, were to have taken the air in the second half of 1970, carrying out route-proving flights to enable Concorde to enter service with airlines at the end of 1971.

This forecast of flight dates so far in advance was supposed to keep the manufacturers' work-force on its toes, but it also helped to sustain the fiction that Concorde's development costs were predictable within the 1965 £370 million estimate. Almost from the outset both programme and costs moved steadily off target. In 1963 and 1965 there had been major design changes resulting in a capacity of 136 seats. In 1967 there was another upheaval, this time to meet airline demands for a better layout. As we have seen, BOAC, Air France, and Pan-American had given advice from the beginning. But in the autumn of 1967 Pan-American and the six other American customers – American, Braniff, Capital, Eastern, TWA, and United – formed a group called the Mentzer Committee, after the chairman of United Airlines, to advise the manufacturers on both Concorde and the American SST. On Concorde their chief demand was for more baggage and cargo space to carry profitable mail cargoes. To meet this, four seats had to go and there was an increase in all-up weight from 350,000lb. to 370,000lb.

The weight increase – the fifth since the project had started – was extremely worrying from the point of view of operating costs, since it signified a further deterioration in the payload-weight ratio. It also raised structural problems.

A structural problem is liable to arise with any aircraft when an increase in the design weight puts extra loading on the wings and other structural members. In a supersonic aircraft the problem is accentuated by the kinetic heating of the aircraft skin. At Mach 2 this approaches the point at which aluminium alloys begin to lose strength. If the Concorde with its new in-creased weight was not to risk metal fatigue before completing its planned life of 45,000 hours flying – the equivalent of more than 12 years active airline operation – the temperature had to be reduced. This meant reducing the cruising speed from Mach 2.2 to Mach 2.05* and increasing the London–New York journey time by five minutes.

While this was not serious from the operators' standpoint, so long as the plane achieved its promised payload and range performance, the reduction in cruising speed was a clear indication that the design weight had reached the maximum permissible. In other words, Concorde, unlike the general run of commercial aircraft, could not be 'stretched' except by a major re-design and at very great cost.

Although the changes in 1965 did not affect the prototypes, work on them fell behind schedule, and when, on 11 December 1967, 001 was ceremoniously rolled out of its assembly hangar at Toulouse on a cold and cheerless day, it was clear that the prototype would not be ready to fly on 28 February. The chief hold-up was in component deliveries from sub-contractors. The French alleged that British firms had failed to meet target dates; the British in turn accused the French of changing equipment specifications and duplicating inspection work that had already been done by the suppliers. On 28 February 001 was still undergoing engine tests. Two months later more time was lost when the Toulouse workers joined in anti-Gaullist political demonstrations. When 001 finally rolled on to the runway for taxiing trials in August, it turned out that the braking system needed extensive modifications. As a result the prototype stayed grounded for the rest of the year, and thousands of British postage stamps printed to commemorate the maiden flight had to be destroyed after mail rates went up on 16 September.

Concorde 001 finally flew from the Sud Aviation airfield at Blagnac on 2 March 1969. After three days' weather delays, which held the world's Press in increasing frustration, André Turcat, the chief Sud test pilot, lifted it off for a 27 minute subsonic flight. It flew with a lowered undercarriage under camera observation by photographic reconnaissance jets and returned to a thunder of publicity. ('Before long eight sleek Pan-Am Concordes will be among the first to welcome you into the new

---

* The figure could be varied slightly in accordance with the temperature of the atmosphere during the flight.

age of flying', said one of the more memorable advertisements in the next day's French and British newspapers.) Three days later 001 went into an unglamorous programme of test-flying that was not to take it beyond subsonic speeds until spring the next year.

The British prototype, 002, was also late. Instead of flying in September 1968 it finally flew, after electrical and tyre troubles, on 9 April, five weeks after 001.

Both delays meant a postponement of Concorde's in-service date, now making it 1972.

In view of the hundreds of engineering problems involved, there was nothing surprising about the time taken to get the two prototypes airborne. In fact a look at the American supersonic programme, then nearing its ignominious end, put the Concorde in a flattering light. But it was wrong that problems that were now described as inevitable in a programme of Concorde's complexity should have been concealed in the reckoning put before Parliament when it was asked to approve the project.

In 1962, when it was planned that the Concorde should enter service in 1967, the development cost had been estimated at £150–70 million. In 1965 the first re-design, increasing the capacity from 90 to 118 seats, had raised this to £275 million, including £50 million to bring the plane up to standard after it received its certificate of airworthiness. In 1966 the figure became £500 million, including £80 million for post-certification development and £50 million for 'contingencies'. In 1968 it was unofficially said to be 'more than £700 million', including the cost of laying down a production line – a necessity that had not been mentioned in the original estimates. Now, in 1969, it was officially given at £730 million, *excluding* production, for which about £100 million would have to be found on top.

Much argument has surrounded these figures, particularly the element attributable to inflation. In 1969 Air Commodore Davis* calculated that accumulative inflation at about 3½ per cent per year accounted for one tenth of the total increase from £150 million to £730 million. Devaluation of sterling in 1967 added £40 million, and the stoppage of work during the

* *The Concorde Affair*, John Davis, Frewin, 1969.

1968 French political troubles £30–40 million. On Davis's calculation, the last two factors were responsible for a 15 per cent increase between 1966 and 1968 and for adding 40 per cent to the 1962 estimate. But the rest of the increase – £340 million, or about 200 per cent on the 1962 figures – was due to design changes and underestimates of time and effort.*

How were such sums (or even a part of them) to be recovered for tax-payers?

In the beginning it had been assumed by the British and French Governments that the whole of Concorde's development costs should be recovered by a levy on the sale of each aircraft. This was quite feasible when the costs were estimated at £150–70 million. Such a sum could have been recovered by a levy of £1 million per aircraft if there were 160 sales (the Government's figure) or £400,000 per aircraft if there were 400 sales (the manufacturer's figure). But with each upward twist of the cost estimates, a realistic levy became harder to contemplate. By 1969 the levy would have had to be £4 million on 200 sales, or £8 million on 100 sales – a figure much closer to the Government's private sales estimate. The Labour Government had early let it be known that it expected to recover no more than one third of the costs. But by the time Labour went out, in 1969, the pretence at recovering a third had been abandoned.

In 1969 the Government's careless financial control of the Concorde programme was exposed in a cost-benefit analysis by Mr C. B. Edwards, a lecturer in economics at the University of East Anglia.

Edwards began by criticizing the Treasury for naïvely swallowing the 1962 development cost estimates provided by the makers. At that time, he pointed out, studies in both the United States and Britain suggested that errors in time and

* In 1969 Mr Wedgwood Benn, Minister of Technology, said that changes accounted for about two thirds of the increase (measured at constant prices) between 1966 and 1969. But Davis doubted that this ratio applied all the way back to 1962. 'Maybe each factor was responsible for half the increase. At all events, the original 1962 figure was clearly an underestimate.' Three years later in 1972 the Government said that of £85 million increase on the £885 million estimate of December 1970, £45 million was for pay and price increases, £25 million for additional development tasks, and £15 million for revision of estimates.

cost estimates of technologically advanced work were usually considerable. American studies showed that the actual costs of 22 projects, mostly in the military sphere, had on the average come out 6.5 times higher than the estimate, while the time taken had been 1.5 times greater, the average time delay being two years. A study of British ventures showed that over a range of about 100 projects, the actual costs had worked out at an average of about 2.8 times greater than the estimated costs.

Had the Treasury made allowance for this pattern of deviation from the manufacturers' cost estimates, and made the appropriate adjustment of the latter to £450 million, they would have found that even with a scale of 200 aircraft there would have been a loss of £208 million on the programme. (Even on the estimate of £150 million for development, there would have been a loss of £8 million!) However, by 1969 the final development cost looked like being about £900 million. If to this was added a jigging and tooling (production) cost of £100 million and a profit per aircraft of £2 million, the net loss estimated on continuing the programme – i.e. after writing off the £380 million spent to date – would be £300 million; half to each country.

As from 1969 the continuation of Concorde was no longer justified on normal commercial grounds but only on the hope of its foreign exchange earnings. What this meant was that if Britain and France sold 200 Concordes for export at about £10 million each, the investment of nearly £1,000 million of public money in the plane's development would produce about £2,000 million in foreign exchange, the sums being divided equally between the two countries. A year later with unit production costs also going up, it began to look as if Concorde would be lucky to sell even the 56 copies represented by export 'options' – especially if the Americans had at last found an answer to the problems they were having with their SST.

At this point, however, Concorde received one of those fillips which seemed to give it a charmed life. On 20 May 1971 the SST, its only serious rival in the supersonic market, was cancelled by a vote of the US Congress.

8. Congress Kills the SST

In a decade characterized by anxious self-questioning among many Americans about their goals and institutions, the American debate on the supersonic transport stands out as a democratic process whose example could be studied with profit by both Britain and France. The forces deployed in support of the SST were greater than any the European aircraft industry could muster; the traditional bias towards technological progress was strong; and the administration was as committed to the supersonic programme as were the British and French Governments. Yet there was a quite different outcome from that of the Concorde debate.

The power given to Congres *vis-à-vis* the Executive under the American Constitution was a central reason but it was not, of course, the only one.

The fact is that the vote which stopped the SST would never have taken place but for the relentless probing for facts about the programme, not only by congressional committees but also by the American Press and conservation bodies, which went to great lengths to master the technical details of the SST project. To anyone studying the record it must also be clear that the industrial interests – both plane makers and airliners – were considerably more frank about their problems than their European counterparts; and if there were recriminations at the time of the cancellation, there must be many in the American industry today who are glad that they did not plunge deeper into trouble.

As late as 1967 the SST's in-service date was still being given as 1974 and Concorde's as 1971. The two planes were not necessarily exclusive - Floyd Hall, the president of Eastern Airlines, said he regarded them as 'stable-mates'; other American airlines said they expected to fly Concorde over 'low density' routes. But obviously Concorde's market was dependent on its lead over its rival.

The history of the SST had been erratic. In the late 1950s, while the Supersonic Transport Aircraft Committee was studying the delta wing in Britain, the National Aeronautics and Space Administration (NASA) had been evolving a series of more complex shapes. In 1963 President Kennedy authorized a development programme with a spending ceiling of $750 million. But as we have seen (Chapter 3) it was not until the middle of 1964 that the Administration sorted out competing designs to the extent of commissioning further studies by Boeing and Lockheed.

The Lockheed design was for a slender double-delta wing. Boeing had gone for a much more daring design – a giant swing-wing designated the 2707. On 31 December 1966 the US

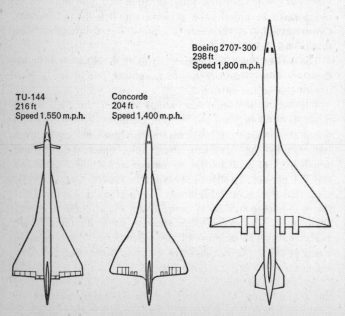

Boeing 2707-300
298 ft
Speed 1,800 m.p.h.

TU-144
216 ft
Speed 1,550 m.p.h.

Concorde
204 ft
Speed 1,400 m.p.h.

Figure 7.

Government announced its choice – the 2707. It was to be powered by the General Electric GE4 engine, which emerged as victor in the competition with Pratt and Whitney.

The Boeing design looked a formidable competitor to Concorde. It promised twice Concorde's seating capacity (250-350 seats), a 25 per cent higher cruising speed (Mach 2.7 compared with Mach 2.2), and a slightly longer range (4,000 miles). But it also had a formidable weight problem. Right from the start officials of the Federal Aviation Administration, which was in charge of the overall programme, had been pretty sure that Boeing had underestimated the empty weight of the prototype. The FAA had therefore stipulated that the latter (which contained no galleys or passenger trappings) should have a maximum weight loading of 635,000lb. This meant an empty weight, without fuel and payload, of about 288,000lb. – a figure that was to be graven on the company's heart.

To make sure that Boeing got its figures right, the FAA encouraged it to spend six months improving the design before submitting it to the FAA and a technical committee of the airlines. The project was put under a special department headed by one of the company's leading supersonic engineers, Holden Withington.

Withington had always been fascinated by the swing-wing concept which had been developed by the British designer Dr Barnes Wallis in the early 1950s. It had been used in the F–111 fighter-bomber, but nobody knew whether it would work in an aircraft as large as the SST. In Withington's design the pivot of the wing was a large 36-inch-diameter titanium bearing, worked by a jack-screw and three hydraulic pistons. With a pivot for each wing, the whole mechanism added about 40,000lb. to the structural weight. This extra weight was supposed to be offset by the gain in aerodynamic efficiency. But it was plain from the start that the balance would be a fine one, because of the low ratio of payload to all-up weight in a supersonic plane.

Withington allowed himself a 3 per cent margin of error, compared with the 7 per cent margin usually accepted in subsonic designs. Even so, in a design for an empty weight of 288,000lb., a 3 per cent error would mean dropping 15 per cent from the payload. As it turned out, the error was much larger.

For six months Withington worked on improvements demanded by the FAA and the airlines. But when the design was put through computer and wind-tunnel tests problems of control and stability appeared. The chief was the tendency of structures such as stabilizers to bend when control power was applied. This meant a loss of efficiency. Increasing the power or stiffening the structures meant increasing the weight; and since the main controls were located in the tail, this produced problems about the centre of gravity.

By early June, when the design should have been 'frozen' for work to start on the prototypes, it was clear that this position was still far off. In fact the whole preliminary design programme had to be changed. Withington now decided to fit a canard or small foreplane to provide better longitudinal control and to extend the tail to improve stability. The canard looked like solving part of the control problem, but required a hydraulic mechanism to move it up and down. This put up the weight again. Fitting it amounted to basic design change, which required FAA approval.

The FAA was extremely unhappy. The design was getting into the weight-fuel-weight spiral. Nevertheless, it approved the canard while warning Boeing that if the prototype reached its now expected weight the aircraft would never be passed for production.

Fitted with the canard, the design became known as the Dash 200. But the makers were unable to do anything about the weight. They continued design work, hoping to solve the problem after the prototype had flown and had proved that the plane could fly at Mach 2.7.

A month after starting design of the canard, Boeing engineers made an alarming discovery. It now turned out that the empty weight of the prototype could reach 360,000lb. – enough to eat up the entire payload. Working against time (they were supposed to 'validate' the design change to the FAA's satisfaction by the end of the year and start cutting metal the following February) the team now attempted to 'sweat out' non-essential weight. Bit by bit, and very, very painfully, they got rid of

23,000lb. – 30 per cent of it by reducing passenger amenities such as seat space and galleys. But the empty weight remained 50,000lb. above the limit.

In September Withington, now pinning his hopes on a break-through in the use of new materials, set up a second team to decide, independently of the existing one, whether the Dash 200 could be saved. It produced some hopeful findings, for example that 20,000lb. could be saved by the use of a new titanium process, but it also warned that there could be no technological improvement in time for the prototype.

The findings obliged Withington to report to his management that the Dash 200's shortcomings could not be overcome except by expensive modifications which the FAA and airlines would almost certainly reject. Two weeks later he admitted that he could not meet the January validation deadline. But worse was to follow.

On 23 October, 28 airlines sent representatives to Seattle for a progress briefing. During this, word slipped out that weight-saving economies had been made in the passenger amenities. The airlines reacted so violently that nearly 10,000lb. had to be put back.

Boeing now reverted to an earlier hope: that the FAA could be persuaded to accept the prototype as a research plane. With this in mind the team worked round the clock to produce a design that was at least stable and controllable. By New Year's Day they seemed to have it. But the weight trouble remained. The empty weight was going to be at least 50,000lb. more than Boeing had agreed with the FAA. This meant that, flying from London to New York with the full projected payload of 300 passengers, the finished plane would run out of fuel about 200 miles short of Newfoundland.

Thus ended any possibility of convincing the FAA of the swing-wing's feasibility, though even now Withington was reluctant to give it up. At the end of January he proposed stopping work on the prototype and asking for time to explore the chances of saving weight by new technological develop-ments and also alternative designs.

The decision went to the Boeing president, William Allen, who decided to ask for another year. The FAA agreed, subject to one condition – Boeing would now have to put $45 million of its own money into the programme.

For the second try Withington used a new design chief, Kenneth Holtby, who had nothing to do with the Dash 100 or Dash 200. Holtby began by comparing the Dash 200 with 16 other possible types, of which three were chosen for final examination. All showed a better performance than the Dash 200, but the one which came out best was a design called the 969–302.

Superficially the 969–302 looked very like the double-delta Lockheed design which had lost to Boeing in the 1964–6 competition. But it differed from the latter in having a broad horizontal tail and broader wingspan. This gave it a better subsonic performance than the Lockheed plane, but slightly reduced efficiency at supersonic cruising speed.

The 969–302 was renamed the Dash 300 and presented to the FAA on 15 January 1969. A special feature was that the fuselage could be enlarged without a major change in wing structure. This would give airlines a choice of payload and range combinations. With seats five abreast, an all-tourist version would seat 234 passengers. A shorter-range version ran to nearly 300 seats. If it was less than 40 per cent full, a 10,000lb. water ballast tank would be used to move the centre of gravity forward.

Compared with the rogue swing-wing, the Dash 300 was a model of simplicity. 'Pure vanilla', was how the FAA supersonic project chief, General Maxwell, described it when it was presented in January. Within six weeks it was officially approved by President Johnson who now gave the supersonic programme his full support. The prototype, with a maximum gross weight of 325,000lb., was supposed to fly in March 1972, and the first production plane (with a gross weight of 750,000lb. in the largest version) to be delivered in 1978. Twenty-six airlines had provisionally ordered 122, in an estimated market for 500. If the estimates were right, the US Government would recover about $1,000 million in royalties – nearly the whole of its share in the development cost, estimated at $1,200 million.*

* The costs would be divided about 2 to 1 between airframe and engines. Up to an agreed limit the costs would be shared by Boeing and the Government in the proportion 10 to 90.

But before the new programme could go ahead Congress had to approve the President's request for dollars: 96 million in the fiscal year 1970, 314 million in 1971, 189 million in 1972, 48 million in 1973, and 13 million in 1974, by which time the basic development would be almost finished. After the swing-wing fiasco, and coincident with a downswing in the economy, it was not the best moment.

Ranged against the SST in Congress were two distinct groups – the 'economists' led by Senator William Proxmire, the Wisconsin Republican dedicated to stopping the outflow of funds to West Coast aerospace companies; and the 'environmentalists', headed by Congressman William Yates, who were more concerned with the threat of the boom, the problem of ground noise, and the risk of atmospheric pollution. The two groups formed an alliance to challenge the formidable aerospace lobby headed by Senator William Jackson, the Seattle Democrat, who had long been known on Capitol Hill as the Senator for Boeing.

The combination of Proxmire and Yates confronted the new President, Richard Nixon, when he took office on 20 January. During the election campaign Nixon had sidestepped every awkward question about the SST by promising that when elected he would 'arm the people with the truth'. One of his first acts in office was to set up an *ad hoc* committee to investigate the facts about the supersonic programme. He then appeared to forget the committee and, encouraged by the FAA, which had fallen for Holtby's 'vanilla', pledged support to the plane makers. The committee report, which dropped on his desk two months later, was a block-buster. After weeks of hearing evidence from both supporters and critics, the 12-man team, handpicked by Nixon himself, condemned the SST on almost every count.

For a start, it doubted whether the volume of sales could ever repay the government investment, if only because the airlines in 1978 would still be paying heavily for their jumbo jets. It also doubted whether Boeing could make both the SST and the 747, whose first prototype was just coming off the assembly line. The problem was production finance. To make the SST, quite apart from the Administration's funding of its development, Boeing would need more than twice the company's net worth. Nor did the *ad hoc* committee see any sign of the big technological 'spin-off' that aerospace interests had said would arise from the programme.

As to the great mass of technological problems involved in supersonic flying, the committee observed that no doubt all of them were *eventually* soluble but the question was: how soon and at what cost? 'The record for new aircraft making technological jumps of this magnitude is confined strictly to military production. The record in those cases is not good. Production costs have often been more than three times what they were predicted to be.'

On the environmental effects of the SST the report was positively scathing. According to the committee's special investigating panel on the subject, the SST was liable to 'intensify hazards to the passengers and crew and cause significant deterioration in the environment for people on the ground, particularly in the vicinity of SST airports and along SST flight paths.' The panel noted four principal problems – sonic boom, airport noise, hazards to those who flew in the aircraft, and effects of water vapour in the stratosphere.

All the available information indicates that the effects of sonic boom are to be considered intolerable to a very high percentage of the people affected. The Panel is cognizant of statements and reports to the effect that supersonic flight over US continental land areas is not contemplated at this time and that SST design and development is proceeding on this assumption. However, the Panel is very concerned about the economic pressures that will be exerted if it is subsequently found that the economic success of the aircraft depends on overland flights at supersonic speed. For this reason the Panel believes that it is essential that the public be formally assured by appropriate authorities that commercial supersonic flights overland will not be permitted and that SST design, development and economic consideration are and will remain restricted to over water routes.

On aircraft noise the panel noted 'a wave of public reaction to aircraft noise' on and near airports throughout the world.

The development of methods to reduce engine noise is an essential element in the development of the SST as well as subsonic jet aircraft. Reduction of engine noise, however, is more difficult for the SST. Acceleration to supersonic speeds and efficient supersonic cruising requires engines with high-temperature, high-velocity jets. These engines are fundamentally noisier than the fan engines that are optimum for the subsonic jets.

After quoting figures to show that the SST would be considerably noisier than the Boeing 707 on the ground, the panel suggested that against the SST

significant numbers of people will file complaints and resort to legal action, and . . . a very high proportion of the exposed population will find the noise intolerable.

The panel drew attention to the greatly increased danger to passengers and crew from any malfunction of the SST at its 65,000-foot cruising altitude. Because of the concentration of toxic ozone, any pressurization failure would result in all aboard losing consciousness within 15 seconds. The hazard from radiation would also be 100 times greater than at ground level, so that a flight crew exposed for 600 hours annually would accumulate 0.85 rem (roentgen-equivalent-man) from this source alone. When this value was compared with the maximum permissible dose of 0.5 rem for the general public, the question arose whether SST crews should be placed in the category of radiation workers and kept under close surveillance. It was also possible that pregnant women, especially in the first trimester, should be precluded from travelling in the planes, said the committee.

Some of these criticisms were later challenged by scientific experts produced by the SST lobby. But they must have been enough to give the President, who had just approved the Dash 300, a nightmare. The report was kept secret for seven months – and only released, as a result of pressure from those who had contributed to it, on 31 October.

On the day of publication, Congressman Yates reminded the House of Representatives that when President Kennedy had launched the SST programme six years earlier he had declared that in no event would government investment be allowed to exceed $750 million. With the appropriation proposed for the current year, the Kennedy limit would almost be reached –

'and if the appropriations scheduled to be made over the next five years are added, the airplane will cost more than one billion dollars more than the amount that Kennedy established. I believe this is the logical time to call a halt to the programme and I shall try to strike the appropriation in my committee.'

To protect the programme from over-close questioning, but also to meet the charge that the FAA had a conflict of duties as sponsor of the SST and guardian of the public interest in safe and efficient air transport, Nixon transferred responsibility for the programme to the Department of Transportation. There it was put in charge of a new 'Office of Supersonic Transport' whose head, a former test pilot, William M. Magruder, had actually headed the unsuccessful Lockheed supersonic design project.

But to get his $94 million the President had still to run the gauntlet of Proxmire in the Senate; and in the hearings on the appropriations request in November Proxmire dragged from government witnesses the damaging admission that commercial considerations might force the SST to be offered for supersonic operations over the United States – a prospect that seemed to be taken for granted by the Administration when television viewers saw President Nixon telling a party of schoolchildren that they would one day be able to travel from Los Angeles to New York in two hours.

For one moment it still looked as if the SST might be saved when its opponents agreed to a compromise resolution that would have deducted a token $11 million from the President's request for funds. But the agreement collapsed in face of an unexpectedly violent reaction by the Press and public, whom the environmental organizations had eagerly educated. It was not merely that (as the *New York Times* put it) 99 per cent of the population would never fly in an SST and expected sonic booms to shatter their peace. It was also a fact that for a vast section of the American population the Supersonic Transport had become the symbol of a multitude of technological ventures – civil and military – pursued at the expense of human needs.

For the final battle the various environmental bodies formed a powerful alliance – the Coalition Against the SST. Typical of its campaign was a large advertisement warning New York newspaper readers that the SST would 'break windows, crack walls, stampede cattle and hasten the end of the American wilderness'. One of its chief targets was the SST's ground noise. The makers had promised improvements that would make it no worse than existing jets. This was beside the point. The Coalition argued that just when the airlines and aircraft manufacturers had at last been obliged to *reduce* existing levels – the SST would reverse this trend.

The makers, who were preparing to build the Dash 300 prototype and hurrying to get out a mock-up, fought back. Against the anti-SST advertisements, *pro*-SST posters appeared, emphasizing the threat to American aerospace leadership if the first SST were to be Concorde, or (worse) Russia's Tupolev. But the aerospace lobby, despite its great resources and the backing of the Administration, was on the defensive.

In May 1971, pulling one of its last tricks, the Administration got the House of Representatives to vote for the $299 million SST appropriation by including it in the general budget of the Department of Transportation, which could not be rejected without halting the entire US road-building programme. The Senate replied by holding critical public hearings on the SST. Among the witnesses called was the eminent economist, Professor Samuelson of the Massachusetts Institute of Technology. Even if the SST had no adverse environmental effects, Samuelson told the Senators, it would be 'an economic and political disaster'.

A few days later the Senate took a final vote on the President's appropriation request and turned it down by 52 votes to 41. But there was a last-minute standstill when House and Senate leaders agreed to fund the project for a further 90-day period pending a vote by a newly elected Congress. Meanwhile Senators' desks were flooded with letters from thousands of citizens mobilized by the Coalition. On 20 May the Senate again voted, this time by 49 to 47, against any more funding. The SST was finally dead.

9. Concordski

While Sud Aviation (soon to be re-named Aerospatiale) was working to cure Concorde's brake troubles, and Withington's men were going through agonies trying to get the SST's weight down, the Russians chose the last day of 1968 to stage the maiden flight of the Tu–144. Alexei Tupolev, son of Andrei Tupolev, creator of Russia's first passenger jet, the Tu–104, had begun work on the supersonic design within months of the 1962 Anglo–French agreement. Its shape, when it was finally unveiled, was so similar to Concorde's that there were speculations that the Russians had copied, or even stolen, the Anglo–French design.

The wing, like Concorde's, was a thin delta. There was Concorde's droop nose and retractable visor, and the general dimensions and projected performance were very much the same. The principal difference was the grouping of the Tupolev's four Kuznetsov engines in a long nacelle below the fuselage. (Concorde's engines were in pairs below the wings.) When a later version of the plane appeared in 1972 even this difference had been modified in favour of a more Concorde-like arrangement.

In 1967 the suspicion that the Russians had obtained secret information about Concorde was strengthened by the arrest of two communist agents who had been operating in the Toulouse area. Evidence was given at their trial about the hiding of microfilm in tubes of toothpaste aboard the Ostend–Warsaw express. A year later two employees of the Kodak company were charged with selling photographic material about Concorde.

But although this seemed to point to a foreign intelligence operation, BAC and Sud Aviation consistently denied that secrets had been stolen. 'If they had been,' said a BAC official, 'the Russians would simply have bought themselves a whole load of trouble that we ourselves were just ironing out.'

The theory now generally accepted is that once the Russians had decided to build in aluminium they were certain to come up with the delta shape that had attracted the British and French. But a certain amount of copying was inevitable. As BAC's Filton chief, Dr A. E. Rusell observed, in commercial aviation the Russians were followers rather than innovators – witness their Tu–134 and I1–62 which looked like copies of the Trident and VC–10.

Whatever the reason, the Russians committed at least one Western blunder. For commercial purposes the Tu–144 was ludicrously small.

The first Western experts to get a glimpse of the Tupolev had been members of a British industrial delegation, including George Edwards and led by the Minister for Aerospace, John Stonehouse, who had visited Russia in 1968. This was to return a Russian visit to Britain the year before. The Russians had seen the Concorde plant at Filton and the Rolls-Royce plant at Derby and had expressed interest in the long, between-overhaul life of British engines. Seeing the half-finished shape of the Tu–144 in the Tupolev factory near Moscow, George Edwards was sure it would not be ready for at least a couple of years. But he was wrong.

The prototype which flew on 31 December 1968 beat the maiden flight of Concorde by two months. It lengthened its lead by a further two months when it flew supersonically for the first time on 5 June. There was then a two year interval before it appeared at the 1971 Paris Air Show at Le Bourget amid rumours that the Russians were intending to sell it to the non-communist world. (Air India was considered the likeliest target because of Soviet–Indian defence cooperation.) There were also reports of plans to start supersonic services to Tokyo and Canada within a couple of years.

The Tu–144 touched down at Le Bourget a day ahead of Concorde on 25 May. It was literally a clean landing because 'Concordski', as the Tupolev was inevitably nicknamed, trailed none of the engine smoke that marred Concorde's landings and take-offs. The pilot, Captain Eduard Elyan, taxied it to the aircraft display area where it was joined next morning by 001 flown up from Toulouse by Turcat. The placing of the two planes only 100 yards apart from each other gave spectators, and particularly Western service attachés, a chance to compare their technical niceties. The Russians, however, refused to admit Western visitors to the interior of their plane until the last day of the show, when General Ziegler made this a condition of allowing the Russians aboard Aerospatiale's 001.

The Western experts were all agreed on one thing. Concordski was less complex than Concorde and showed signs of having been built rather quickly. At least one Western expert thought it had a centre of gravity problem because of its relatively crude wing section. To achieve balance when it went into supersonic flight it looked as if it would be necessary to transfer large quantities of fuel. Even this seemed insufficient to produce a sensitive enough trim condition because there were control surfaces running the full span of the wing, which could create a supersonic penalty.

Nearly everyone criticized the arrangement of the air intakes which seemed liable to suck in runway dust and debris. There were also signs of makeshift modifications, such as a large-diameter fuel transfer pipe running externally to the tail.

On the third day of the show the Russians gave a press conference in the trade cinema. The start was delayed until someone was found to stop the projector which was showing an extremely boring film about the making of French engine components Elyan was introduced, and talked enthusiastically about the handling of the plane. But when an official of the Aviation Ministry invited questions. Elyan was not able, or not allowed, to answer the most basic questions about the test flying programme. Nor could officials say anything about arrangements for marketing the plane. Western reporters came away with the impressions, which later events confirmed, that the Russians had hurried to get the Tupolev on show for prestige reasons but that, like the makers of Concorde, they had a long way to go before putting it into service.

But on one point the Russians were probably a trick ahead – their decision to power the Tupolev with the Kuznetsov turbofan engine. Allusion was made in Chapter 3 to the supersonic designer's basic choice between the turbofan type of engine and the turbojet type with its noise problem. Now is the moment to say more about the difference between the two types and the design of the turbojet in particular.

The turbojet consists of an air intake, a compressor, a combustion chamber, a jet pipe, and an exhaust nozzle. The compressor supplies high-pressure air to the combustion chamber for the burning of fuel. It is driven by a shaft from the turbine, whose blades are turned by the expansion of hot gases in the combustion chamber. The main difference in the turbofan (see Figure 8) is that a fan is used to blow additional *cold* air to the back of the engine to slow down the jet stream for greater subsonic efficiency. This also reduces the noise.

In high performance turbojets such as the Olympus 593 additional fuel may be burnt in the exhaust area by injecting into it the oxygen that remains surplus from the initial combustion. This is known as re-heat (or in America after-burning). In Concorde it is switched on to accelerate the plane to its supersonic cruise speed. While this is happening another process is taking place at the front end of the engine, i.e. the air intake, which is perhaps the most crucial component of the whole supersonic power-plant.

With a supersonic turbojet the function of the air intake is to slow down the air to subsonic speed, which is the maximum speed at which it can be handled by the compressor. It does this by using the drop in air speed which occurs behind a compression shock wave. Depending on the speed to be absorbed, anything up to five shock waves can be created by using the various arrangements. In the intakes of Concorde's Olympus engines this is achieved by a system of moveable ramps which are controlled automatically according to the Mach number. The electronic control for this system is housed in an air-conditioned equipment bay and is crucial to the aircraft's efficiency and safety.

One of the problems resulting from the intake arrangement is the rise in the temperature of the air as it is forced to slow down. At Mach 2.2 it enters the engine at about 153 degrees centigrade. With the temperature increase that then takes place in the compressor and combustion chamber, this produces a

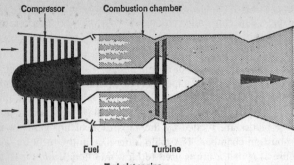

Compressor   Combustion chamber

Fuel   Turbine

Turbojet engine

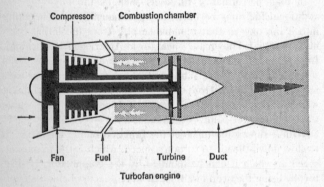

Compressor   Combustion chamber

Fan   Fuel   Turbine   Duct

Turbofan engine

Figure 8. The turbojet (top) puts all its air through the combustion chamber to produce a high-speed jet which is most effective for supersonic flight, but extremely noisy. The quieter turbofan (bottom) passes part of the air through ducts outside the compressor and combustion chamber; this air then mixes with the hot gas of the jet, cooling and slowing it down for efficiency at subsonic speeds.

temperature of about 1,000 degrees when it enters the turbine stage – 200 degrees higher than in subsonic engines. This calls for the use of special materials in the turbine blades and other high-temperature parts. It also presents a challenge in respect of the reliability of the engine, which to operate commercially is required to run for up to 5,000 hours between overhauls, half the time supersonically, compared with, say, 15 hours supersonic running between overhauls by highly advanced military engines.

In their preoccupation with temperatures and noise (to which we shall turn presently), it was perhaps not surprising that the makers of the Olympus should have overlooked the problem of its engine smoke. All engines emit a certain amount of smoke at landing and take-off. But the clouds trailed by Concorde were strongly criticized when it overflew the 1970 show at Farnborough. After this Rolls-Royce engineers designed a new type of combustion chamber to consume the unburnt fuel residues. But at the 1971 Paris show the new 'annular' combustion chamber had still to be incorporated. The only way to reduce the emission of smoke by the prototypes was by additives to the fuel. This was adopted when, on VIP day, the heads of customer airlines, including BOAC and Pan-American, were taken aboard 001 for a flight across the Bay of Biscay. All went well until Turcat switched on the re-heat. It was then found that the engineers had put in too much additive after critical comparisons with the smoke-free Concordski. The after-burners failed to ignite and the party returned without having flown supersonically.

10. Why BOAC Resisted

By 1971 no airline wanted supersonics though none dared admit that it was opposed to 'progress'. The grounds for refusing to take them were contained in a list of requirements that had been drawn up by IATA back in 1962. These stipulated *inter alia* that the supersonic aircraft must be competitive with subsonic aircraft operating at the time of its introduction. This meant, in IATA's own words at the time, that:

(1) No increase in the level of engine noise can be tolerated. In fact, engine noise must be lower than that of subsonic jets operating at present, in order to permit round-the-clock operations.

(2) Economic operations at supersonic speed must be practicable over habited areas at any time of the day or night.

(3) Supersonic seat-mile costs must be equal to or better than those of subsonic jets of comparable size and range operating at the time of its introduction.*

The position of BOAC and Air France was particularly difficult. Both had been repeatedly consulted over Concorde's specifications and were expected, as state airlines, to place the first orders for the plane. Any hesitation in this matter would be taken as a sign of low confidence in Concorde. Pan-American was also in a special position because of its privileged contract and its place above the 13 other customers on the overseas delivery list.

The conditional basis of all airline options on Concorde was its performance 'uphill' from Paris to New York, a distance of 3,628 miles, against prevailing winter headwinds. In 1962 the guaranteed payload had been 90 passengers; in 1965 it had been increased to 118, and in 1967 to 128-32 passengers. Because of the shorter distance between London and New York (a difference of 172 miles) Concordes flying the Atlantic from London

* For the full list of requirement see Appendix p. 157.

would have a 'bonus' of 3,000lb., enabling them to carry four more passengers.

When it was first announced, this increased payload, which was supposed to be available within two years of Concorde's entering service, seemed to satisfy the airlines, which were then comparing Concorde with the Super VC–10 (174 passengers) and Boeing 707–320 (189 passengers). For Concorde was able, in return for its high investment cost, to fly two trips to the subsonic's one. But with the coming of the Boeing 747 the basis of comparison suddenly changed; and with it the attitude of the airlines.

Another event that changed airline attitudes was the demise of the American SST. The SST had been scarcely more popular than Concorde, and for much the same reason. But at least so long as no one knew the final purchase price, it could be supposed that with 300 seats and slightly longer range it would be marginally less uneconomic. When the SST failed, the hopes of other supersonics fell also. And, despite the triumphal cry of Aerospatiale's General Ziegler that this meant a golden opportunity for Concorde, the order book remained dead to the day that BOAC and Air France were obliged to place orders by their governments.

The first of many reports that BOAC was less than happy about Concorde had appeared in the British Press in 1963. Like subsequent ones it was denied with the faultless statement that 'provided Concorde does the job, we are flat out for it'. A year later a rebellious voice was heard in Air France when its UK manager, M. J. de Genner, rashly volunteered that Labour's proposal to re-examine the plane was 'realistic and, in the long run, a good thing'. This brought from Paris the crushing declaration that the *general management* chose the company's aircraft, and that its position could not be reflected by one of its agents – a declaration, which, as *The Times* observed, accorded with the French Government's intention that the onus of any cancellation should be borne entirely by Britain.

The bitterness that developed between BAC and BOAC over Concorde was started by a row that followed the appointment in 1964 of Sir Giles Guthrie, a 48-year-old merchant banker, to take over the chairmanship and put the Corporation's affairs in order. As a condition of his appointment, made by Julian Amery, Guthrie demanded that the Government write off BOAC's accumulated deficit of £80 million, largely incurred by the patriotic buying of British aircraft, and issue it with a clear directive to 'operate as a fully commercial undertaking'. Part of the deal, for which BAC never forgave Guthrie, was the cancellation of the greater part of BOAC's order for the Vickers VC–10, with which BAC was hoping to cut into the long-haul jet market.

From the operators' point of view the trouble with the VC–10 was that it had been designed for take-off from short runways. This was in the belief, back in 1958, that the Boeing 707 would not find sufficient long runways in the Commonwealth. (The cheap expedient of extending the runways was overlooked.) Because of its take-off capability the plane had higher operating costs than the 707, but its special capability was not needed.

BOAC had been talked into ordering 42 VC–10s – 12 in the 'standard' version and 30 in the longer-range 'Super' version – because the makers could not afford a smaller production run. Guthrie slashed this to seven 'standards' and 20 'Supers', simultaneously cutting back BOAC's inflated fleet plan from 62 to 39 big jets. If ever BAC had a chance of selling the VC–10, which is doubtful, it was now gone. From now on BAC was ready to pounce on the first hint that BOAC might be 'doing a VC–10' on Concorde.

Guthrie was suspected, not without reason, of being sceptical about Concorde. Though he avoided prejudging the plane in public, he was aware of its operating penalties; and when the list was opened for options on the larger and hopefully more economic American SST, in 1964, he caused a furore by putting BOAC desposits on six aircraft. (The signing of the contract had temporarily to be held up while Julian Amery smoothed BAC's feathers.) During 1965 and 1966, when other airlines' sales offices, but not BOAC's, started bristling with Concorde models in company colours, Guthrie again came under fire. In the end relations were so strained that the Labour Government, under pressure from BAC, ordered BOAC to show some enthusiasm.

Guthrie capitulated. In April 1967 at a Sydney press conference to mark BOAC's new 'westabout' service to Australia, he treated correspondents to a picture of the routes that BOAC might operate if Concorde met its requirements. Assuming delivery in 1971–2, he said, Concorde would fly London–New York–San Francisco–Honolulu–Fiji–Sydney–Singapore–Bombay–Beirut–London, and vice versa – 'a round-the-world journey in $27\frac{1}{2}$ flying hours chasing daylight some of the way'. Then with gentle irony, which not all appreciated, he added a postscript: 'After Concorde, ahead of us are the hypersonics, in which we shall be travelling at 5,000 miles per hour.'

In 1967, as Concorde's intended delivery date receded further into the future, BOAC placed orders for the Boeing 747. Sir Giles now dwelt on the luxuries the wide-bodied jets would offer, particularly to first-class passengers who (he might have added) might prefer them to narrow supersonics. It had already been announced that with the outlay on 12 747s, and possibly supersonics as well, BOAC would be saying goodbye to profits until the late 1970s. Twelve months later, in preparation for what looked like being a highly competitive era, it drew up plans for a fleet consisting entirely of 747s, which would simplify engineering problems and reduce overheads.

To those responsible for executing the plan, Concorde was an embarrassment. But after the VC–10 row BOAC had promised not to do or say anything that would look like pouring cold water on Concorde. Thus in a vital period, when BOAC's criticism might have alerted the public to the truth about Concorde's economics, the Corporation – and for similar reasons Air France – was obliged to stay officially silent. It was left to Pan-American to prick the bubble.

In 1969 the president of Pan–Am (and former head of the FAA), Najeeb Halaby, had defended the American SST on its deathbed. Failure to support it would risk the future of America's leadership in aviation, he had told Congress. But now that the SST had been cancelled and Pan–Am was heading into the red, along with other airlines caught by the fall in air traffic growth, he was not going to put on an act for Concorde.

Halaby staged his exposé dramatically in May 1971, during a visit to Concorde's French production base by a party of

American Congressmen, businessmen, and airline executives, sponsored by *Time* magazine. At the Air France headquarters building in Paris the guests were regaled with a sumptuous lunch and some well-chosen words by the *Time–Life* president, Henry Luce III. Concorde was a magnificent aeroplane that would bring the world closer together, Luce assured them (hastily disclaiming that *Time* was in any way engaged in artful salesmanship). The party had come simply to bring 'praise, affirmation, and perhaps an order book or two'; the excitement of its visit would be heightened 'not only by the novelty of seeing Concorde itself but what it symbolizes of the future – and what it implies for the spectrum of that future which we trust will be broad and varied and highly coloured'.

Halaby now rose and, before anyone realized what he was doing, proceeded to deflate Luce – 'bringing some cold oxygen into the euphoria', as he himself put it. After praising the Concorde as a 'tour de force' – 'one of the most fabulous stories of forced technological growth in the history of man' – he observed that, comparing it with the giant Boeing 747, passengers might nevertheless find flying in Concorde a bit 'old-fashioned', like going back from the living room to travelling in a tube.

He then revealed Pan-Am's doubts, shared with BOAC and Air France, about Concorde's high operating costs and small capacity, and stopped just short, before a thunderstruck audience, of proposing that the plane should be cancelled. In the long run, he said, the British and French would have to face a tough question – were they prepared to produce a very limited number of Mark I Concordes and then face up to planning and financing a Super-Concorde, 'an airplane that will better meet the requirements of both passengers and airlines'? It was wonderful to hear Ministers talk of Concorde as a vehicle of entry into the Common Market, but if it were that, surely a large part of the development cost could be written off as the entry fee?

In their book, *The Battle for Concorde,* Costello and Hughes relate that, after Halaby sat down, Geoffrey Knight, Chairman of BAC Filton Division, icily remarked, 'I feel something warm and wet trickling down my back.' 'That was no knife,'

Halaby is said to have interrupted, 'that was a needle, and it was aimed lower than your back.'

Another needle was applied a few months later when Halaby suggested that the airlines interested in supersonic operations should jointly own and operate a 'trial fleet' of Concordes for a period of years in order to get experience of the plane.

BAC saw this as an attempt to get Concorde stopped, which it probably was, because Halaby must have known that it would be impossible to re-start production after a halt, and that the unit production cost of the 'experimental fleet' would be colossal.

Later still Halaby suggested that the United States, Britain, France, and 'perhaps the Soviet Union' should get together to build the 'Super Concorde'; and in a presidential letter to Pan-Am employees he wrote:

I must tell you that I have serious reservations about the present version of the Concorde – about its noise, and social acceptability, whether we can make money on it, about whether it is fully reliable . . . It may be that if BOAC and Air France exercise their options, we'll wait as long as we possibly can while they fly it in commercial service before we make our decision.

This too was seen as an attempt to sabotage although Sir George Edwards himself had suggested that the United States and Europe should explore the possibility of supersonic co-operation.

In the meantime a report highly critical of Concorde had been submitted to the board of another American customer, United Airlines*. Dated 1 March 1971, it contained the conclusion that: 'economics clearly militate against acquisition of the Concorde.' The section written by the airline's economic planning division – one of five divisions contributing – said it could not see how Concorde could operate profitably over United's 2,000-mile trans-Pacific route between the American West Coast and Hawaii. Assuming an all first-class service and a $26.5 million (£12 million) purchase price, 'Concorde requires

---

* Quoted in the *Observer*, 25 May 1971. On 11 June the *New York Times* quoted critical comments from the presidents of two other US customer airlines – Robert F. Six of Continental and Howard C. Wiser of TWA. Hardly any of this criticism was reported in the British Press.

a 50 per cent surcharge over the first-class fare and a 60 per cent annual average load factor to obtain a 10.5 per cent return on investment.' Concorde could be considered only as an all-first-class aircraft, the economists warned. If it were split into the same proportion of first and economy passengers as United's 747s 'a load factor of 160 per cent would be required to return 10.5 per cent.' The marketing division described Concorde's fuselage as 'a fast DC–3 tube' with Spartan passenger facilities, and said it could not support a continued commitment.

The report disclosed that United had twice considered ending its options on the plane, but that the makers had persuaded it to let them continue. It had done so only because the price had now increased so much that the company could withdraw from the programme later without financial penalty.

From mid 1971 onwards the idea of the Super or Mark II Concorde – which would rescue the programme from the terrible blunder about size – began to loom increasingly large in BAC's thinking about sales prospects. But it could not be talked about publicly because, as a BAC official admitted, 'first, there are no funds for it and, second, if you say there's a Mark II coming along, nobody's going to place orders for the current model.'

In the meantime BOAC and Air France were faced with becoming compulsory buyers of the Mark I. The chairman of BOAC was now Keith Granville, whose long service, beginning as a 10-shillings-a-week clerk with Imperial Airways in 1929, inclined him to place emphasis on the Corporation's mandate to 'operate commercially'. His problem with Concorde was that he did not even know whether the plane would meet its performance guarantees (which would still leave it greatly inferior to the latest subsonic jets on payload range and noise).

The guarantees were an explosive issue. When BAC's first draft contract reached BOAC in 1971 it was remarked that if it had come from any other manufacturer, BOAC would have thrown it into the waste-bin. It contained no safeguards in the event of inadequacy, nor could the makers give clinching evidence, on the basis of flight tests, that the plane would do all that was promised of it. This, however, was contrary to the picture presented to the public by BAC, which in January

1971 had assured the Press that Concorde had come through supersonic performance tests with flying colours.*

The performance question was to revive shortly. In the meantime there were critical uncertainties about supersonic air routes. Would Concorde be allowed to fly supersonically over important land areas? Would it be granted round-the-world landing rights? Would it be allowed to land at New York even? Would the Americans, who were not keen on the safety aspects of aluminium supersonics, accept a British certificate of airworthiness for the plane?

The question of routes could not be settled without international agreements which the Government had yet to negotiate. So BOAC had to work on hypotheses, with the additional problem of not knowing what proportion of air travellers would be ready to pay a supersonic surcharge, at a rate not yet fixed, for the sake of flying faster in an aircraft whose amenities, other than speed, were inferior to those of wide-bodied subsonic jets.

From 1969 to 1972 BOAC fed its computers with a variety of assumptions about fares, performance, and operating costs in an effort to discover which routes would support a supersonic service. Most of the answers were discouraging, particularly those relating to the North Atlantic, for which Concorde had been expressly designed.

The problem was the timetable Concorde's 'productivity' depended on its being able to make four transatlantic crossings a day, but, as Bo Lundberg was to demonstrate in a paper to the Council of Europe†, Concorde could achieve this only by departing and arriving at some highly unpopular times (and severely restricting the time available for maintenance). Statutory restrictions on night jet landings were another limiting factor. The result was a typical transatlantic timetable as follows:

* On the strength of BAC assurances, I wrote in the *Observer* of 24 January, 'Tests began last April and have taken the aircraft to speeds of Mach 2. They have shown that the Concorde can carry at least 25,000lb. or about 128 passengers and their luggage between Paris and New York.'

† 'Bo Lundberg Report 147', presented to the Committee on Social and Health Questions on 6 July 1971.

Westbound
Dep. London 08.30 Arr. New York 07.00
Dep. London 18.30 Arr. New York 17.00

Eastbound
Dep. New York 08.00 Arr. London 16.00
Dep. New York 22.00 Arr. London 06.00

With such a timetable the only glamorous flight was the early morning westbound flight, which would enable businessmen to do a day's work in New York and return the same evening. The afternoon flight was less satisfactory. It would merely get passengers to New York in time for dinner (which they would already have taken in the air). The eastbound flights were positively inconvenient. In order to catch the 8 a.m. flight, passengers would have to rise about six and would arrive in London in the afternoon rush hour. The overnight flight would be unrelieved torture; it would deposit the traveller, after a sleepless night, at London Airport at six in the morning. No hotel would be ready to receive him; nor could he decently telephone friends. The best he could do would be to breakfast at the airport while the subsonic traveller took breakfast in the air before landing at a sensible 9 a.m.

As for the 'day return' trips, these were much less glamorous when seen in relation to the passenger's physical condition.

Businessmen flying to New York for the day would put in at least seven hours waking and travel time before meeting their American opposite numbers at the start of the New York day. Throughout the day they would be more tired by at least five hours than the Americans. On returning home (at about 8 a.m.) they would have been up for at least 25 hours (allowing for the time spent in airports and on the ground journey) and would be totally unfit for work the same day. As for 'day returns' in the opposite direction, these would be virtually impossible because of the time difference and night-landing curfews.

Assuming only limited competition (from Pan-Am and TWA) BOAC calculated that the most the North Atlantic would support in the high season would be two Concordes, and in the winter only one.

The Corporation now looked at its Far Eastern and African routes. BAC had regularly claimed that the 27-hour Sydney–London journey would be cut to 13½ hours; but this was optimistic. Even if the Australians granted supersonic corridors – booming 'a lot of kangaroos and a couple of Abos', as BAC's Press chief, Charles Gardiner, gaily put it – it would still be necessary for 'sea-limited' Concordes to fly south of the populous islands of Indonesia in order to reach Singapore, and then south of India to reach Dubai in the Persian Gulf. Concorde would then have to fly subsonically across the Middle East. All this could take nearer to 20 hours than 13½ and the £200 round-trip surcharge was likely to rule it out for all but a few executives.

In the end BOAC decided that there might be enough traffic to support three Concordes a week, but since nobody was going to wait up to 48 hours for a supersonic flight, when subsonic flights were leaving daily, the three-flights-a-week service was not on.

This left two other routes where Concorde might be used – a route to the Far East across the Soviet Union (which was one of the few countries thought likely to permit supersonic overflying, because of the Tu–144) and the route to South Africa.

The South African route was found to be profitable if Concorde could refuel at Lagos. It carried a high proportion of first-class passengers and had no problems about night landings. The route across Russia required fuelling stops at Moscow and at a point in Siberia, possibly the town of Norilsk, which nobody from BOAC had ever visited. It too could be profitable, but this depended on the Japanese Government allowing Concorde to land at Tokyo, which in turn could depend on Japanese public opinion (which was vocal about the environment) and perhaps on the ordering of Concorde by Japan Air Lines.

There is no doubt that in 1970 BOAC, faced with Concorde's operating costs, the problem of integrating it into its subsonic fleet, and the uncertainty about its routes, was ready to say no to the plane. By so doing it could have brought the project to an end. But its memories of the VC–10 row made it cautious. It believed that cancellation was the duty of the Government, and that the Government's knowledge of Concorde's economics would lead it to the right decision.

As we shall see, things turned out otherwise on the advice of Lord Rothschild. In that situation there was only one thing Granville could do – agree to order Concorde on condition that the Government underwrote the losses.

11. The Pollution Debate

For many of its critics the case against Concorde turned entirely on its impact on the environment. Its economics were irrelevant, except insofar as the whole vast expenditure might have been put to better use. Among those who felt this way were a few who believed that its most serious consequence might not be the boom, or even its engine noise, but the damage resulting from the intrusion of kerosene-burning aircraft into the hitherto unpolluted upper atmosphere.

In April 1970 a leading American scientist, Dr Harold Johnston of the University of California, Berkeley, reported to President Nixon that a world fleet of 500 supersonic transports could halve the ozone content of the atmosphere in less than a year. If this happened, all animals in the world would be blinded if they lived out of doors in daylight – and some of Dr Johnston's colleagues at Berkeley believed that all plant life would die as well.

The basis of Dr Johnston's frightening prediction was the amount of nitric oxide contained in the supersonic transport's exhaust. This, he explained, could set up a series of chemical reactions that would seriously deplete the ozone layer that protects all forms of life from the lethal ultra-violet rays of the sun. One of the effects of human beings would be to increase the incidence of skin cancer.

These risks had been dismissed earlier by atmospheric chemists, who said that the effect of nitric oxide would be small. One of their arguments was that nitric oxide produced by industry, motor cars, and subsonic aircraft was already 'leaking' into the atmosphere without any noticeable effect on the ozone layer. Johnston demonstrated that his thesis already took account of this process. What had so far prevented the contamination of the stratosphere, he explained, was that the stratosphere (upper atmosphere) was isolated from the troposphere (lower atmosphere) by the ozone layer itself. As the ozone absorbed ultra-violet it was heated, with the result that the stratosphere was warmer than the air below. Since the lower air was cooler, there was no convection effect, and the ozone acted as a kind of lid.

This lid was penetrated only very rarely, said Johnston, mainly by thunderclouds but more recently by high-flying aircraft such as the SR-71 spy plane. Commercial jets and most military aircraft were designed to fly at an altitude of 5-7 miles. But supersonic transports would fly much higher in order to take advantage of reduced resistance from the thin upper air.

Now, ozone exists mainly between 10 and 30 miles above the earth because of a balance of chemical reactions continuously creating and destroying it. Above 30 miles the ultra-violet rays of shortest wave length are absorbed by oxygen gas – a process in which the oxygen molecules are split into individual oxygen atoms. The surviving rays then enter the 10–30-mile high region where ozone absorbs the remaining lethal wave lengths. In this last process the three-atom ozone molecules are split into oxygen gas molecules and individual atoms; but at the same time the ozone is replenished by a reverse action in which single oxygen atoms merge with two-atom oxygen molecules to form ozone – an action requiring the presence of some other atom or molecule to act as a catalyst.

Johnston pointed out that nitric oxide would rob ozone of one oxygen atom, converting it into oxygen gas, which cannot serve as a complete ultra-violet shield. In this reaction the nitric oxide becomes nitrogen dioxide, with two oxygen atoms, but another reaction quickly converts it back into nitric oxide. *It thus becomes available to attack another ozone molecule.*

In this way, according to Dr Johnston, the exhaust of supersonic airliners at 10 miles or more altitude would wipe out virtually all the ozone in the lower atmosphere. The nitric oxide would then slowly diffuse into the higher levels of the ozone region, and this process could not then be stopped even if the world took alarm and stopped the supersonics from flying.

As the *New York Times* pointed out*, Johnston's prediction of what would happen if the ozone was sharply depleted depended on theoretical knowledge of the role of ozone itself in heating the atmosphere and keeping it isolated from the turbulence below. There were difficulties in using laboratory findings to determine what would happen in the atmosphere, whose conditions were difficult to reproduce and not fully known. Nevertheless, his argument was a reminder that some of the factors that make the world habitable for all forms of higher life are fragile: 'Their care and sustenance must be mastered before we endanger their survival – and our own.'

Another phenomenon that caused alarm among some scientists was the supersonics' output of water vapour. The matter was first raised by Dr V. J. Schaefer, a distinguished atmospheric physicist and director of the Atmospheric Sciences Research Centre at Albany, New York. In 1968 Schaefer suggested that 400 SSTs, discharging something like 150,000 tons of water vapour daily in the upper atmosphere, might produce 'global gloom'.

This was because the weight of water released in jet engine fuel combustion is about 40 per cent greater than the weight of fuel consumed. Since the American SST, on which he based his reckoning, was expected to burn 280 tons of fuel in four transatlantic crossings a day, Schaefer calculated that the 400 SSTs could daily release an amount of water vapour equal to 0.025 per cent of that produced naturally in their altitude range.

This additional water vapour could produce persistent vapour trails, leading to a marked increase in cirrus cloudiness and in

* 'Sorry but there's still more to say about the SST', 30 May 1971. At a conference on aero-engine pollution held in London two years later a British meteorologist, Mr Philip Goldsmith, advanced the argument that nuclear tests in the atmosphere produce quantities of nitrogen oxides comparable with those that would be produced by large fleets of SSTs. But when the record of nuclear testing was compared with the record of ozone concentration, he said, there appeared to be no connection whatsoever. Professor Johnston sharply contradicted this in a letter to the London *Sunday Times*. He said Goldsmith had totally miscalculated the temperatures resulting from nuclear-bomb shock waves, because he had not realized that the chemical reactions involved were endothermic, i.e., required energy to go on. This gave a vast overestimate of the nitric oxide expected. 'The problem of stratospheric ozone and its vulnerability to supersonic transports remains an unsolved problem,' said Johnston.

the relative humidity of the atmosphere – both of them effects that could upset the radiation balance and possibly the general circulation of atmospheric components.

Schaefer calculated that if half the supersonic activity were concentrated over the North Atlantic air routes, the resulting contamination could be ten times greater than that calculated on a global basis. Subsequent studies contradicted this picture by indicating that vapour concentrations would spread out and lose their significance. Nevertheless it was agreed that they remained a matter for investigation when more was known about horizontal mixing times in the stratosphere and the time that gases reside there.

Another geophysical effect disregarded by the Anglo–French and American supersonic transport programmes was the inordinate demand that supersonic fleets would put on world oil supplies. The matter was raised in an article in the *Observer* on 30 August 1970, with the result that the newspaper was attacked by Magruder's Supersonic Transport Office.

The article pointed out that if the sales targets set by the makers of the Concorde and the Boeing SST were ever realized, they would contribute to a critical oil shortage by 1985. It went on:

The British Aircraft Corporation says that one Concorde will consume 18,600 gallons on a 3½ hour London–New York flight. To justify investment in the aircraft, airlines will have to operate four transatlantic flights by each plane each day – or an average of 14 hours revenue flying in every 24. This means that a single Concorde will consume 272 metric tons of kerosene daily. Over one year the consumption amounts to an astounding 100,000 tons.

If, as planned, there are 300 Concordes in service by 1980, these planes will burn 20 million tons of kerosene in that year. With the addition of 80 Boeings (due to come into service from 1978 onwards) the total annual consumption by the entire supersonic fleet in 1980 will reach 46 million tons. But to produce one ton of kerosene means refining at least seven tons of crude oil. The 1980 Supersonic fleet will take up 322 million tons of unrefined petroleum. *International Petroleum Encylcopaedia*: North Africa, 1,120 million tons; Western Europe, 1,100 million tons (UK, 144 million); Soviet Bloc, 710 million; Latin America, 240 million; South-East Asia, 200 million; Africa, 95 million.

These figures are based on projections of how international oil requirements for industry, motor transport, domestic heating, and the chemical industry are likely to grow.

They allow for the enormous expected growth of air traffic (currently about 12 per cent per year) but cannot take account of the further vast increase that would be occasioned by a switch to supersonics, whose production still requires British and American government approval.

The critical factor is that the supersonics consume up to two-and-a-half times as much fuel per passenger-mile as subsonic aircraft, and are ultimately expected to carry about 20 per cent of all traffic. In 1990, for example, there are expected to be 600 transatlantic crossings a day by supersonics, compared with 200 by subsonic airliners if the latter are all 'jumbo'-sized jets.

To meet the increased demand, the oil industry is currently planning to double its production in the next decade – from a world total of about 2,000 million tons this year to 4,100 million tons in 1980.

Tanker tonnage, refinery capacity and well-head production must double in the next ten years to meet these demands. Whether the oil industry can do this is doubtful.

By 1985, the combined Boeing and Concorde fleets will need around 11 per cent of currently projected world oil demand, and very much more than the requirements of several under-developed continents.

All this suggests that the £2,000 million that will ultimately be needed to launch the Concorde and the Boeing could be more rationally applied to the development of technologies that will ease, not aggravate, the transition to a world without oil.

Three weeks after the *Observer* article appeared, the US Office of Supersonic Transport Development issued a statement saying that 5 per cent of projected crude oil production was 'more than adequate to supply all civilian jet fuel demands up to 1985' and added that by 1990 the entire American SST fleet would use 70 million tons of oil. But these figures appeared to be based on a much lower supersonic fleet figure than the makers' estimates and applied only to the American plane. Since then the difference between subsonic and supersonic fuel requirements has further widened due to design changes and supersonic fuel demands have again become a subject of inquiry because of the world energy crisis.

Although these geophysical threats were potentially the most serious ones while America's SST was still being built, what worried most people in Britain was the down-to-earth menace of Concorde's ground noise and the sonic bang.

In September 1970 the British-assembled prototype, 002, began supersonic test-flights down the west coast. These flights were not to test public reaction – the route was dictated by the need to be within range of radar and rescue services – but the results in terms of damage were revealing.

Up to 6 January 1972 (when the flights were still continuing) there were 20 flights, of which 11 crossed Pembrokeshire, eight crossed Cornwall, and 19 crossed western Scotland.

For the period in question the Government was obliged to pay out £25,239 in damage compensation, of which £13,933 was for damage to buildings, £10,853 was for injury to animals, and £452 for 'miscellaneous' damage. None of the areas subjected to the boom was heavily populated, yet in Cornwall there was £50 worth of damage per mile per flight.

In 1968 and again in 1972 Bo Lundberg raised the question of sonic bangs over *water*, and particularly over North Atlantic shipping lanes.* This was something nobody else had investigated.

Lundberg explained that horseshoe patterns of super-bangs would be caused off busy coastal areas such as New York, Boston, and the Bristol and English Channels, because of the focusing effect of the plane's initial acceleration beyond Mach 1. People aboard passenger ships, freighters, pleasure boats, and fishing vessels in these areas could expect up to two sonic bangs an hour, including occasional super-bangs in the 3-4 psi overpressure range. Even greater overpressures could result from multiple reflections of the shock-wave from a ship's thick plate-glass windows.

Lundberg pointed out that every supersonic crossing of the North Atlantic could 'boom' an average of about 4,000 people. It was unlikely that shipowners and crews would accept this situation, he argued, because of the annoyance and because of

* 'Acceptable Nominal Sonic Boom Overpressure in SST Operation over Land and Sea'. Paper presented 14 June 1968 to the National Conference on Noise as a Public Health Hazard, American Speech and Hearing Association.

the danger of bangs striking crew members balanced on the superstructure during maintenance operations. Before cancellation of the SST the American magazine *Space Aeronautics* published a map which suggested that 80 per cent of the North Atlantic would be blanketed by bangs. This was because eastbound and westbound air routes would be spaced about 100 miles apart and because supersonic aircraft would be serving widely separated cities on each seaboard.

Many people divined that on over-water booms Lundberg was addressing a very small audience; if supersonic transports actually came into service the best one could hope for was probably a prohibition of supersonic overflying until aircraft were a minimum distance from land – say 50 miles – which would spare most yachtsmen and inshore fishermen. But as Concorde strove for sales there were growing fears that commercial considerations would lead to permission for regular flights over land areas also.

In 1970 the Labour Government had published a White Paper on the environment that effectively promised a ban over Britain – but it went out of office before legislation could be introduced. Switzerland banned supersonic overflying in 1968, and Sweden in 1972. Canada and Japan both announced bans about the same time. In 1971 the new Conservative Government said that it was reserving its freedom of action on the matter. The French Government already permitted regular overflying by military supersonic aircraft and intimated that it would allow the same to Concorde. What would America do? This was the key question.

In May 1972 the Federal Aviation Authority published a proposal to ban the sonic boom over United States territory, but not to ban supersonic overflying as such. This meant that aircraft would be permitted to fly at speeds up to about Mach 1.15, at which it was possible for suitably designed aircraft to avoid creating a bang on the ground. The concession meant little to Concorde, which at Mach 1.15 used 25 per cent more fuel than at Mach 2. But it suggested a place for a boom-free *transonic* aircraft, for which both Boeing and Lockheed had done various studies. In 1973, however, the FAA changed its mind and banned supersonic flights absolutely, except in test areas.

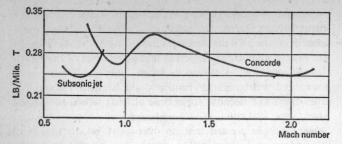

Figure 9. Fuel consumption at various speeds. The sharp increase between Mach 0.9 and Mach 1.4 makes it uneconomic to decelerate temporarily over populated areas on the flight route.

At no time did the plane-makers find any ground for hoping that the boom could be eliminated. When it was suggested in 1967 that the supersonic shock wave could be reduced by ionizing the plane's leading surfaces, a Boeing executive, Mr William Hamilton, pointed out that no aircraft could be expected to generate the amount of electric power required. All efforts to reduce the boom below Concorde's and the SST's 'normal' level of 2.3lb. per square foot overpressure had been fruitless, he told a meeting of the American Institute of Aeronautics. The same year the US National Academy of Sciences said a drastic reduction of the boom appeared to be impossible, at least with current designs, though there might be 'small improvements' through refinement of aerodynamic design, propulsive efficiency, and operating procedures.

A similar situation emerged with regard to engine noise.

Concorde's noise problem begins with its wing shape. Designed for efficiency at twice the speed of sound, this is much less efficient than conventional wings for developing lift for take-off. As a result, Concorde needs a very high take-off speed which it gets from high-thrust engines with very high jet velocity. (Proportionately to take-off weight, Concorde had 63 per cent more thrust than the Boeing 747.) This high thrust is provided by the reaction between the air and the mass of hot gas expelled from the exhaust nozzle. The greater the exhaust velocity, the louder the roar as the plane takes off and climbs to cruising altitude.

On landing approach another problem occurs, for as Concorde reduces speed, the drag of its sharply swept wings actually *increases*. To compensate for this, the thrust on landing, too, has to be greater than for subsonic aircraft and the engine must be given frequent bursts of power.

As explained in Chapter 9, the problem with Concorde's engines is that they are turbojets and not turbofans. In the latest turbofans it is possible to cut noise spectacularly by having three times as much air by-pass the combustion chamber as goes through it. This, however, requires a very large nacelle. In subsonic engines the drag from the nacelle is more than offset by the turbofan's lower fuel consumption. But in supersonic aircraft the drag is too great. American engineers are now seeking to develop a 'two-phase' engine which would combine the characteristics of both turbofans and turbojets and which, if successful, could bring an acceptable supersonic transport somewhat nearer.

Another constraint on noise reduction in the Olympus is the re-heat system. Because it requires a varying gas flow, re-heat rules out the fixed-diameter silencing nozzles that are possible with subsonic engines. Faced with this problem, the French engine partners, SNECMA, developed a retractable 'lobe' type silencer for aircraft operation. But its inadequacy was brutally shown up when Concorde made a bad weather diversion to London after flying over the Farnborough Air Show in 1970. As the plane roared in over the suburbs of Barnes and Richmond, thousands of people rushed to their doors, alarmed at the shattering noise. The perfect landing by the pilot, Brian Trubshaw, demonstrating that Concorde could fit into the subsonic traffic pattern, did not assuage the wave of indignation. The airport switchboard was jammed with telephone calls, one from a man who had had the tiles shaken from his roof.

Three days later BAC officials said that the production Concorde would be fitted with more effective silencing devices. This was a new type of silencer that had been on SNECMA drawing boards since the spring. It consisted of spade-shaped scoops that were lowered into the jet stream to cause mixing between the high velocity exhaust gases and some low velocity secondary air that flows between the engine and the nacelle. This would cut noise by reducing the overall velocity of the jet exhaust and by setting up turbulence in the jet stream.

Another device announced at this time was known as TRA (Thrust Reverser Aft). Mounted aft of the silencer, the thrust reverser – primarily to act as a brake on landing – could be opened to allow air to be drawn in and mixed with the jet stream, reducing the overall jet velocity, and therefore the noise, still further.

In the summer of 1971 the makers were promising a 6 PNdB noise reduction by means of these two devices, and a still greater reduction later on. But many experts doubted whether this further reduction would be possible without fitting a multiple silencer to divide the jet stream. This would entail a performance penalty, which would be extremely serious in view of the low ratio of payload to declared usable fuel load.* There was also some doubt about reaching the basic targets now set for the production aircraft. On 24 April 1972 Mr Geoffrey Holmes, Chief Public Health Inspector for Windsor and Technical Director of the Noise Abatement Society, took a noise measurement of 002 as it returned to Fairford after visiting the Hanover Air Show. His meter, placed at the standard measuring point one nautical mile before touchdown, registered 131 decibels, compared with the usual 115 decibels for a VC–10 or Boeing 707. It was calculated afterwards by the Anti-Concorde Project that, even allowing for a 5-6-decibel reduction by spade silencers and TRA, plus a six-decibel 'trade-off' in converting PNdB to EPNdB†, the production Concorde's approach noise would be at least 12 EPNdB above that of the latest subsonic jets, and at least 7 EPNdB short of the declared target.

After demands by MPs for official figures, the makers' noise targets compared with the noise levels of subsonic aircraft were given by the Aerospace Minister, Mr Heseltine, in the House of

* See article by J. L. Goldberg, in *Search*, the journal of the Australian and New Zealand Academy for the Advancement of Science, vol. 3 no. 3, March 1972. Goldberg pointed out that a 1 per cent increase of fuel consumption would mean a 7 per cent cut in payload.

† EPNdB (Effective Perceived Noise Decibels) differs from the simple PNdB measurement in that it reflects variations in the time that the aircraft may be in the vicinity.

Commons on 4 May 1972. The figures, on the EPNdB scale, were:

	Take-off (flyover)	Approach
Concorde	114	115
Boeing 707–320C	114	120
Boeing 747–100	111	114
Boeing 747–200	108	109
VC–10	110	115
Lockheed 1011	98	103
DC–10	99	106
Trident III	104	110

This list was based on types of aircraft that would be flying when Concorde was supposed to enter service in 1975. The difference it admitted between the Concorde and the DC–10 and Lockheed 1011 Tri-Star was startling. But without reference to the logarithmic character of the decibel scale the full extent of this difference could not be appreciated.

A better guide to Concorde's position in the noise league had been published 10 months before by the British Airports Authority. In three diagrams, which are still the most valid official document on Concorde's noise, and which are reproduced as Figures 10, 11 and 12, on pages 114-16, the Authority gave take-off, approach and side-line noise levels in a form that converted the decibel scale into a linear measure. The BAA diagrams also included, what Mr Heseltine's figures conveniently left out, the noise level of the Boeing 707 and other noisy aircraft when fitted with acoustic devices ('hush kits') to reduce mechanical and jet noise.

These diagrams showed that on every count – take-off, approach and side-line measurement – Concorde has double, or more than double, the noise level of the DC–10 and Tri-Star. These are the aircraft that by the end of the decade will be carrying the bulk of the Western world's medium-haul traffic. (As from 1972 a level some 45-50 per cent below Concorde's noise targets has also been achieved by the new series Boeing 747, which within a few years will be carrying the greater part of long-haul traffic.)

CF–8

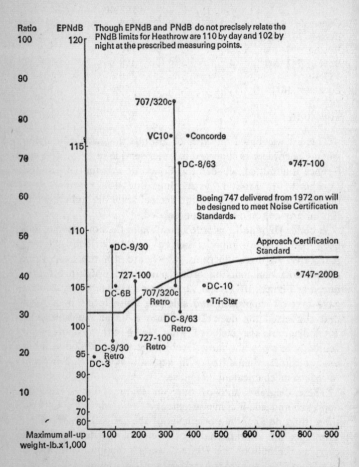

Figure 10. Approach Noise Levels (1 nautical mile from threshold on the extended runway centre line).

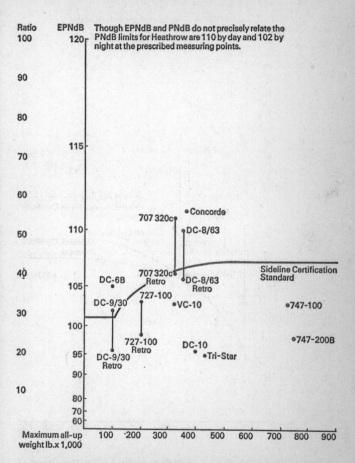

Figure 11. Side-Line Noise Levels. At a point on a line parallel to runway centre line – 3 engines and less 0.25 nautical miles; more than 3 engines 0.35 nautical miles.

115

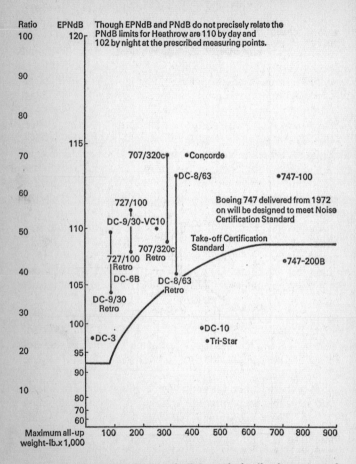

Take-Off Noise Levels
(3.5 nautical miles from start of roll on extended runway centre line).

Figure 12. Take-Off Noise Levels (3.5 nautical miles from start of roll on extended runway centre line).

Yet another fact highlighted by the BAA diagrams was how far Concorde would exceed the noise limits set for all new British aircraft by the Air Navigation (Noise Certification) Order of 1970. The Order specifically excluded Concorde and other supersonic transports from these limits for the simple reason that there was no foreseeable means of silencing it sufficiently. But there was no reason why other countries should be so obliging.

Apart from these documented figures, there were other aspects of Concorde's noise output that were going to cause trouble as the makers tried to sell it around the world. One was the calculation, readily made by any airport authority, that since Concorde had only a third to a quarter of the jumbo jet's passenger capacity, it would be forced to create three times as many take-off and landing disturbances in order to carry the same number of people. In other words, on a per passenger basis, it would cause *six* to *eight* times the noise of a Tri-Star or DC–10.

Another point emerging from a study of its noise measurement was that the EPNdB method, being partly based on the *duration* of the noise emission, favoured the Concorde in relation to subsonic jets because of its quicker take-off (which was no consolation to anyone woken by the Concorde as it passed noisily overhead). Another possibility, suggested by sensationally high decibel recordings during Concorde operations at Fairford and later in Australia, was that the EPNdB measurement, being the mean of a series of fluctuations, did not reflect the very loud surging required of Concorde's engines during landing.

These matters, like the actual achievement of the noise targets, remained to be proved or disproved by the production aircraft. The makers affirmed that there was *no* insurmountable noise problem. But the plain fact was that the Concorde, which would make flying noisier, was being thrown on a world that had just decided to make it quieter.

12. The Point-of-no-return Myth

A persistent theme running throughout the history of Concorde, the argument by which it was most frequently rescued from the fate which a realistic appraisal of its economics demanded, was the argument that it had 'passed the point of no return'. It had first been made in the winter of 1964 when the Labour Government was persuaded that it would cost more to cancel the programme than to get out of it. Thereafter it was used in every debate about Concorde, and appeared to gain strength from each new announcement of the total of funds invested. It was always a specious argument, because no serious attempt was ever made to calculate the consequences of withdrawal – and because the costs of continuing were essentially open-ended.

In 1964 the cancellation of the programme would have entailed the joint writing off about £200 million; but as matters turned out, it would have saved at least £800 million. In 1968 the investment written off would have been £400 million, the saving at least £600 million. Two years later, at the end of the Labour Government's term of office, when the financial commitment had reached £500 million, the point-of-no return argument seemed to have gained more force. But again it was false, because even if the development costs were finally to be contained within the then current estimate of £825 million, which proved not to be the case, there would still be the cost of *producing* the aircraft. This would have to be reckoned as a loss unless large quantities were sold – and by now the Government was being advised that sales of more than 60-70 aircraft were out of the question.

Mr Heath's Government, which took over from Labour in 1970, was the spiritual heir of the Macmillan administration which had started Concorde nine years before. But there were differences of style. The new Prime Minister prided himself on a 'modern' approach. One of his first gestures was to broaden government by the recruitment of leading figures in industry. Another was to set up a Whitehall 'think-tank' under the Labour peer and scientist, Lord Rothschild, to study long-term national problems and coordinate measures for their solution. Heath himself knew little about technology. But he made important decisions in the course of devolving power to those who did. In the new Government, aircraft production was put under the overall direction of the Minister for Trade and Industry, John Davies, who also had ultimate responsibility for BOAC and BEA. Within a few weeks Davies – a former oil chief and ex-chairman of the Confederation of British Industries – announced that the Government was not going to rescue any more 'lame ducks'.

The Government had three lame ducks on its hands, of which only one was immediately recognizable – Upper Clyde Shipbuilders, whose collapse had provoked Davies's statement. The others were Rolls-Royce, whose impending bankruptcy was known only to a few people, and the Concorde, which was now three years behind schedule and 300 per cent over its cost estimates.

The Rolls-Royce drama had begun in 1968 when Rolls landed a contract to build the engine for the Lockheed Tri-Star. It was the biggest order in the company's history, a potential £1,000 million export coup. For two years Rolls had fought to wrest it from General Electric and Pratt and Whitney, knowing that unless it engined an American aircraft it would lack the cash flow for research and development necessary to stay in the big league. Unfortunately Lockheed knew this too; so Rolls was forced to sign a contract at rock bottom price, with high penalties for non-performance and virtually no allowance for rising costs. The engine, the RB.211, was to be twice as large as any Rolls had made, and had to be built in half the time. It would also be an 'advanced technology' engine, with three concentric turbine shafts instead of the usual two, which would make it much quieter than existing engines and cut the number of parts by 40 per cent. Another refinement was the use of a new material – carbon fibre, with the trade name 'Hyfil' – in the turbine blades. This would save 300lb. weight on each engine, a vast saving over the years. Civil servants were faintly uneasy, because Rolls had a passion for perfection and often scant regard for costs and time. But the Labour Minister of Technology, Anthony Wedgwood Benn, was persuaded to back the project by reports from his technical and financial advisers.

Although the RB.211 had a better social image than Concorde (it promised to reduce aircraft noise, not to increase it), the two projects had one factor in common. Both were the product of British determination to get even with the Americans. In the case of Rolls-Royce the resentment went back to 1961 when American Airlines, under pressure from American aero-engine interests, had turned down a Rolls engine for the Boeing 727.

The RB.211 was intended to recapture this lost opportunity to dominate the market when existing engines neared the limit of their development potential in the early 1970s. Rolls, who had had vast success with their post-war civil engines, particularly the Dart and the Spey, did not doubt their ability to do it. In March 1968 they put the engine launch costs of the RB.211 at £65 million – £45 million more than they had put into the Spey 10 years earlier. This was a gross underestimate. By November 1970, when the Government agreed to an urgent request to put in more money, the costs were £135 million, and by January 1971 £170 million. The engine was then nearly 12 months late, and each one delivered to Lockheed would bring a loss of £111,000 on the contract sales price of £350,000.

The problem was Rolls's over-optimism about its ability to build a revolutionary engine quickly. To meet the Lockheed deadline, parts were put into production without being properly tested, and modifications escalated. In the summer of 1970 Hyfil blades, experimentally fitted to a Conway engine in a Super VC-10, disintegrated in a hailstorm over West Africa. Hyfil had to be abandoned. Fortunately Lockheed had insisted on a parallel version of the engine with titanium blades, but these had a weight penalty. Disaster followed disaster till, on 22 January, the Company delivered the shattering news that it would be unable to deliver to Lockheed by the deadline. Four days later it declared itself insolvent.

If the Government had stuck to its lame-duck policy there is no doubt that the RB.211 would have been abandoned. Indeed for several weeks this is what looked likely to happen. But the lame-duck policy was already being modified by the spectre of mass unemployment due to the general recession and the Government's deflationary measures. For a time it looked as if Ministers were faced with the choice of saving the RB.211 (and 30,000 jobs) at an estimated cost of about £100 million, or going ahead with Concorde (and 20,000 jobs) at a remaining cost of about £250 million. Both were commercially unprofitable projects; but the money required to finance the RB.211 was considerably less than that still required for the Concorde. At the end of March the Government, which had already bought up the Rolls-Royce aero-engine assets to preserve their future defence production, gave the guarantees necessary to save the RB.211 – and in August a reluctant Congress approved a similar operation to save Lockheed, which had been almost as close to bankruptcy as Rolls-Royce.

In the meantime the Prime Minister had put the question of Concorde to the Whitehall think-tank. For the next two months Lord Rothschild and his analysts examined the costs of continuing the programme, the benefits likely to come of it, and the penalties of cancellation. By all accounts the final result was somewhat equivocal. Rothschild told Heath that Concorde would never provide a return on the money that still had to be put into it, but that it ought to be continued because of the international implications. He said that, even if sales reached 60, which many thought an optimistic figure, there would still be a loss on production. However, the cost of continuing – about £250 million – was worth paying for the sake of entry into the Common Market.

On the strength of this analysis, the Cabinet decided that Concorde should go ahead and that, to muster as many sales as possible, it must be given solid government backing. One of Heath's first actions was to agree to fly in the plane. (His reluctance to do so had caused comment.) The other was to sack the Aerospace Minister, Frederick Corfield, who had accepted a Departmental estimate that Concorde would sell only 30 copies. In his place he appointed the young and swinging MP for Tavistock, Michael Heseltine, who had been a member of the Conservative Party's Transport Committee. Heseltine's task – to get Concorde sold to the airlines at no matter what price – was regarded in Whitehall as something of a political *kamikaze* mission. Corfield received his telegram of dismissal while talking with Concorde's French makers in Toulouse.

For years it had been an article of faith with BAC salesmen that the first firm order for Concorde would unlock the door to sales of 250 or more. But not even the optimists expected an overseas customer to place an order (or to be allowed to do so by the British and French Governments) before orders had been placed by BOAC and Air France. Thus, although high-powered missions were dispatched to potential new customers in China and Iran, BOAC remained an essential first buyer.

BOAC had earlier decided that, if Concorde was to be cancelled, it should be the Government, and not the Corporation, that bore the odium of the aircraft industry. It had therefore maintained publicly that it *wanted* Concorde, provided that – in Keith Granville's ingenuous phrase – a way could be found of operating it profitably. When the Government decided to go ahead this formula became a useful bargaining counter.

From the autumn of 1971 discussions were pursued with great urgency by the Government, whom BOAC could virtually hold to ransom. This situation was not altered by the setting up, on 1 April 1972, of the new British Airways Board, which was to act as the 'parent' of both BOAC and BEA, and which would actually buy the aircraft.

The Corporation put its demands on the table. If the Government was telling it to order Concorde, it must absolve it from its mandate to operate commercially or else underwrite it against losses. These would arise through Concorde's high operating costs, the organizational problems of a mixed fleet, and the loss of traffic from subsonic services, which would still have to cater for first-class passengers. It would require guarantees against losses due to inadequacies in performance, or the grounding of Concorde by a major engineering failure, or the refusal of countries to grant landing or over-flying rights. It would also need generous help in meeting the purchase price.

The negotiations dragged on throughout the spring, fraying tempers. Parallel negotiations between Air France and the

French Government were even tetchier: the performance of the first batch of Concordes, which were supposed to have a minimum guaranteed payload, flying westbound from Paris to New York, of 20,000lb. (to be increased to 25,000lb. within two years of entering service) could not be established to the airline's satisfaction. Air France was therefore obliged to reduce the capacity of its transatlantic Concordes to 104 seats, compared with the original 128. The problem did not affect BOAC which, because of the shorter distance between London and New York (3,456 miles compared with 3,628), was still able to plan for a capacity of 114.

Another difficulty for Air France was the thinness of the traffic on its projected routes to the Far East and Africa. It could not justify buying even the reduced number of aircraft being considered by BOAC.

The British Aircraft Corporation, anxious for firm orders that would justify a government go-ahead for more production aircraft, hoped first for an announcement in time for the Hanover Air Show in March, and then, when this failed to materialize, for an announcement by BOAC and Air France during a visit by the Queen to France in April. 'A Royal Flush of Concordes' proclaimed a *Daily Express* banner headline: Britain and France were to order five each. But the Royal visit passed uneventfully.

A new, more imperative deadline was now set by a government announcement that 002 was to make a sales tour of 13 countries in the Middle and Far East. The tour was to start on 4 June, and enough was said by Ministers to indicate to BOAC that if it had not ordered by then, it would be letting the side down.

On Thursday 25 May the BOAC orders were finally announced at a news conference at the Airways Board's headquarters in Victoria. The chairman of the Board, David Nicholson, said he was placing orders for *five* Concordes – not the eight on which options were held. The Government was to advance the Board £200 million on public capital terms – that is to say without liability to interest unless and until the Board showed an operating profit in accordance with a sliding scale. Part of the money was reserved for BEA's impending purchase of the Tri-Star. The rest – about £160 million – was for

BOAC's purchase of the Concordes, which would cost £23 million each, including spares and back-up equipment.

The purchase price was shattering; but so was BOAC's compensation. At current rates of interest on the market £160 million was equivalent to a subsidy of about £11 million a year.

The most remarkable thing about the BOAC 'order' (apart from the Corporation's relinquishing three options) was that it was unaccompanied by any announcement from Air France. Nor was it a *signed* order. The settlement of details would take another seven weeks. Only when the ink was dry and Air France had also signed an order would the clock start ticking for Pan-American, which would then have to confirm or terminate its options within six months.

The proposal for the Far Eastern tour had been sourly received at Fairford, where it would interrupt the flight test programme. There was also the risk of a mechanical failure. But the long flight went without snags. 002 was accompanied by two RAF transports, a Britannia and a C–130, carrying spares, including a spare engine, 100 engineers, sales executives, and what the chief test pilot Brian Trubshaw happily called 'hangers-on'. At Teheran, the first demonstration stop, the Shah announced that Iranair was ready to place three orders (later modified to two and an option). This was a bonus, since Iranair was not even an option-holder. In Tokyo Japan Air Lines were reported to be ready to increase their three options if given a higher place on the delivery list. But there were no other positive results. In Australia QANTAS said it could not make a decision without performance data from the second pre-production aircraft, which meant waiting 18 months. In India both demonstration flights were unavoidably cancelled, and it was felt that Air India was backing down.

Back in Britain, after the 45,000-mile journey, visiting 11 countries and clocking up 62 flying hours, of which 23 were supersonic, Concorde was the subject of a congratulatory Press conference. It had, said the Aerospace Minister, Michael Heseltine, ceased to be simply a prototype and had become an aeroplane which thousands of people had seen for themselves, and which they now knew flew like other aeroplanes but at more than twice the speed.

Brian Trubshaw said that its fuel consumption over tropical sectors had been better than expected and that, subject to further experience, it seemed likely that the makers could offer a better guaranteed range and payload performance.

General Ziegler, who had flown with the plane from Toulouse, said that Air France would place its much delayed order 'within a few weeks'. The order, for only four aircraft, was placed in mid July.

But what mattered now was American orders for the plane. While Concorde had been touring the Orient, American customers, and particularly Pan-American, had been fairly uninhibited in talking to the Press about its payload limitations and staggering price.

In July Air Canada announced cancellation of its four options, giving as its reason high operating costs and limited range and payload. Shortly afterwards United Airlines lapsed its six options, specifying most of the reasons that had appeared in the analysis that had found its way into the *Observer* a year before. But the great drama of the option battle, on which everything hung, was not to come until the end of the year.

13. Pan-Am's Bombshell

The crucial date for Concorde's American orders was 31 January. This was the deadline for Pan-American to convert its seven* options. TWA, with six options, was required to make its decision in the following six weeks. The remaining American option holders – American Airlines (6), Eastern (6), Continental (3) and Braniff (3) – were supposed to convert their options within the year.

On at least three occasions in the previous year senior executives of Pan-Am and TWA had criticized 'currently proposed' supersonic transports (by which they had meant Concorde) in papers to national aviation bodies. They had expressed concern about its operating costs, range, payload, noise levels, passenger attraction, and, since July 1972, its price.

BAC must have known of these American views – its contracts provided for continuous consultation with option holders and it had a US-based subsidiary to keep an eye on such things. Yet it persisted in believing that fear of an Anglo–French monopoly following the BOAC and Air France orders would force the American airlines to follow suit.

What it overlooked was the hostile reaction of American airlines to the salesmen's claim to know more than they themselves did about airline operation, and to the makers' ill-concealed boast that they had manoeuvred the sleepy Americans into a corner.

So confident was the makers' tone that, when on 14 January I flew to New York to discover the position and report on it for the *Observer*, I half expected that Pan-American was going to let its arm be twisted. It was my second visit to America in less than three weeks. On 26 December I had gone to Washington at the invitation of Senator Proxmire to give evidence

* It transpired that the eighth option had been cancelled when Pan-Am revised its contract in the previous September.

on Concorde to the Joint Economic Committee of Congress. I had told the Committee, which was investigating moves to re-start the American supersonic programme, that Concorde was a 'political' aeroplane, that it was grossly uneconomic, and that it could hardly be a threat to the US aerospace industry. I had then given my own analysis of BOAC's position but it was only now that I could hope to know the final decision of the Americans.

My talk with Pan-American took place on 17 January on the 46th floor of the giant Pan-Am building overlooking Fifth Avenue. The official I spoke with was a senior member of the company's board, and within five minutes it became startlingly clear that Pan-Am had decided *not* to buy Concorde.

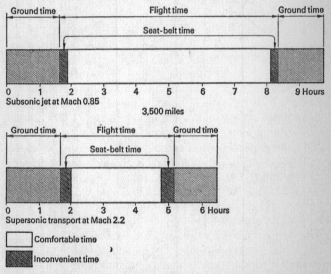

Figure 13. On a 3,500-mile flight, such as London–New York, Concorde's time-saving is reduced in significance by the time spent in travel to and from airports and on the ground. In addition, supersonic passengers must spend longer strapped in by their seat belts while the plane climbs to cruising altitude and later descends. This reduces the proportion of 'comfortable' time. The diagram, by Bo Lundberg, assumes a one-hour journey to and from the airport and 40 minutes at the airport itself, including time in the aircraft.

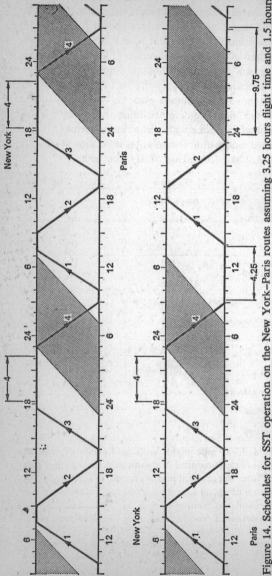

Figure 14. Schedules for SST operation on the New York–Paris routes assuming 3.25 hours flight time and 1.5 hours turn-around time. The upper figure illustrates that 4 single flights per 24 hours would allow a daily maintenance time of only 5 hours, i.e. 1.25 hours per flight, which is deemed insufficient for a longer period. A subsonic jet with a flight time of 7 hours would allow a daily maintenance time of 7 hours, i.e. 3.5 hours per flight. Reduction of the average daily number of SST flights to 3, as shown in the lower figure, would yield an average daily maintenance time of 9.75 hours, i.e. 3.25 hours per flight. Shaded sections represent night hours when taking-off and landing is normally restricted by a noise curfew.

It appeared that the management had subjected Concorde to five criteria which had been the basis of all previous aircraft purchases by the airline. These related to its speed, range, service capability, passenger comfort, and seat-mile operating costs in comparison with existing planes. I was told that the management's assumptions made had been 'extremely conservative', i.e. it had assumed that there would be a low level of competition from other Concorde operators, high passenger load factors, relatively stable fuel costs, and optimum performance by the aircraft. It had also assumed – what was subsequently found to be impossible – that Concordes on the North Atlantic service would make four crossings in every 24-hour cycle. Environmental problems had played no part in the analysis, I was told; not because the economic factors were sufficiently conclusive by themselves.

All this accorded with my own understanding of Concorde's economics and I had no reason to doubt that Pan-Am would act on it. But there was still the possibility that the airline might be persuaded to *extend* its options – a deal which, in default of an order, would be desperately sought by BAC in order to preserve the credibility of its sales campaign with other customers.

When I put this to the Pan-Am representative, he said an extension was out of the question. The company had already spent too much time on Concorde. It could not allow its executives, analysts, pilots, and engineering staff to go on indefinitely evaluating an aircraft which, it was already clear, was quite out of line with the company's needs. I then asked what would happen if the makers were to offer a drastic reduction in price, or perhaps a leasing arrangement by which Pan-American would be subsidized in the same way as BOAC.

There was a moment's hesitation before I was told: 'Even if there were a *drastic* reduction, I doubt if we should find it a commercially viable airplane.'

I was told that the views of the board were unanimous, but that by the terms of the company's agreement with BAC, there could be no adverse announcement until the options expired at the end of the month. Before then the decision to cancel had to be formally registered at a board meeting, which would take place on Thursday the following week.

Next day I talked with a member of the TWA board. Because of its contract TWA was under less pressure for a quick decision. It could wait to see how Pan-Am jumped and would obviously be influenced by the Pan-Am decision. If Pan-Am said No, it could freely follow suit. On the other hand it might be tempted by the reduced sales price and privileged customer position that would then certainly be offered it by the makers.

Yet it quickly became clear that TWA's analysis of Concorde's economics was, if possible, more damning than Pan-Am's. For example, it believed that, because of scheduling problems and the inconvenience of arrival times in Europe, Concordes might be restricted to *two* crossings a day on the North Atlantic.

Another factor to which TWA attached great importance was the rise in the price of jet fuel, of which Concorde would burn four times as much per seat mile as a comparable subsonic jet. Since 1971 the price of jet kerosene had risen some 30 per cent. It was expected to treble by the mid 1980s – the mid point of Concorde's design life – and TWA and other airlines were already looking hopefully to the end of the century for a hydrogen-based substitute.

Apart from these objections (on the strength of which a TWA senior vice-president had been quoted to me as saying that TWA would not take Concorde even if it were offered free) there was a feeling on the TWA board that the supersonic transport had a low priority against other demands on investment resources, such as the need to improve ground transportation and terminal facilities.

I found an equally critical attitude when I talked with a senior executive of American Airlines, which, since the cancellation by United, had become the leading domestic option holder. The American executive told me: 'Our contract was made when we planned operations to Japan. When the Federal Government withdrew permission to operate this service, our requirement for Concorde ended. I have made this quite clear to the British Aircraft Corporation.'

The same situation was revealed in a long-distance telephone conversation with a board member of Continental Airlines in Los Angeles. I was told that Continental had 'ordered' Concorde in 1965 for its proposed service to Australia; permission for this too had been withdrawn. The only reason the company had kept up its options was to be able to compete with Pan-Am if the latter decided to operate Concorde between Los Angeles and Hawaii. This, however, was a remote possibility since the Hawaiian traffic consisted almost entirely of holiday-makers on a cheap-fare basis.

The odd airline out was Braniff.

Braniff had continued to be a vocal supporter of Concorde long after other American airlines had begun to show cool. In addition to a flair for publicity (its jets fly in a variety of eye-searing colours) the airline has over-water routes from New York and the West Coast to Panama and South America which, because of a high element of first-class business traffic, are as near ideal for Concorde as is possible.

But even Braniff sounded cautious when I tracked down its New York public relations chief in the company office in the Chrysler building. He told me there could be no question of confirming options until the airline received definitive performance data, and that even if these proved satisfactory, Braniff's initial requirement might be for only one Concorde.

All this was a very different picture from that still being presented by BAC in London.

The problem about reporting the situation was that, although the Pan-Am board's decision had effectively been taken, it would not become official until after the Thursday board meeting and could not be announced until the options expired on the last day of the month.

Before then a BAC team was coming to New York for what everyone but themselves must have recognized as a hopeless last-minute sales bid. The salesmen's line had been disingenuously leaked to the Press, together with the information that before being put to Pan-American it was tried out on 18 January at a gathering of 70 Wall Street financiers who were expected to put up funds for purchases.

The meeting was addressed by Geoffrey Knight, who told the bankers that Concorde was not an expensive and glamorous luxury but an airliner of the future, capable of making substantial profits for those shrewd enough to buy it. 'It is an aircraft', said Knight, 'that no airline can afford to be without in the mid 1970s.'

Knight's argument was that, although regular full-fare paying now took only 29 per cent of airline seats sold, they still brought in 40 per cent of airline revenues. If American airlines wanted to retain their share of this market, Concorde was the only way, he said. He then produced figures comparing Concorde and the Boeing 747. According to these, Concorde's total seat-mile operating costs were only 60 per cent greater. The result, according to BAC, was that Concorde could break even with 37 passengers whereas the 747 needed 165. Revenues were put at 11 cents per seat mile for Concorde and five cents a seat mile for the 747.

These figures did not convince Wall Street. In particular the comparison of *total* operating costs was contrary to normal practice in the assessment of aircraft, since it permitted the inclusion of an arbitrary share of airline overheads and was subject to manipulation. Using the normal basis of direct operating costs (fuel, crew, maintenance, depreciation) Wall Street's airline analysts agreed with Pan-American's estimate that Concorde was at least 2.5 times more expensive to operate than the latest subsonics.

On Saturday 20 January I filed a story which the *Observer* carried next day under the headline 'American Airlines Turn Down Concorde'. In it I took care to explain that the Pan-Am decision was to be formally confirmed at a board meeting the following week and that the official announcement would not be made until 31 January. I predicted the cancellation of options by TWA and all other US airlines, except perhaps Braniff, within a few weeks.

In London the story caused a furore. BAC heard of it as soon as other newspapers received copies of the *Observer*'s first edition soon after six in the evening. By midnight I had received a call from London, saying that the makers were 'flatly denying' the story.

This was understandable. Sir George Edwards was flying to New York the following day (when I was returning to London) and was still so out of touch as to believe that a deal was negotiable.

On Tuesday Sir George had a meeting with the Pan-Am president, William Seawell, who had meanwhile been obliged to issue a statement that the airlines had not yet taken a decision. The Edwards–Seawell meeting was discouraging; Sir George departed incognito for the West Coast immediately afterwards, leaving the unfortunate Geoffrey Knight to fight a lost battle under the continuing illusion that Pan-Am were merely trying to get the price down.

There my own part in the matter would have stopped if it had not been quite gratuitously publicized by the Minister for Aerospace.

On the Monday following publication of my story, the Member for Bristol South-East, Mr Wedgwood Benn, asked Mr Heseltine a parliamentary question by Private Notice, inviting him to make a statement about the Pan-American situation. In reply the Minister said that the manufacturers hoped to 'convert their options into firm orders' and that they were in 'detailed negotiations with Pan-American'. Mr Benn then thanked the Minister for the reply which he said 'obviously satisfied us that statements which appeared in the *Observer* yesterday were quite untrue'.

As Bernard Levin remarked in *The Times* afterwards, matters might have been left there, with Mr Benn being proved foolish only a few days later. But Mr Heseltine felt he had to go further.

'I can confirm', he said, 'that the statements made in one of yesterday's newspapers to the effect that negotiations had come to an end were a fabrication.'

Next day Mr Heseltine was given a chance to save himself from the appalling trap of his own creation, when the Opposition aviation spokesman, Mr Will Rodgers, suggested that he might like to withdraw what he had said – 'since the implication that the story had been falsely contrived would be a grave reflection on his ethics as a responsible journalist'.

But Mr Heseltine went boldly on:

'. . . there was only one paper that carried a story that Pan-American had decided to cancel its option, and that was the *Observer*. As the Chairman of Pan-American, Mr Seawell (sic), has said that he intends to make a statement about the decision later this month, and as negotiations are proceeding, the evidence is overwhelming that the story in the *Observer* is a fabrication. As the honourable Gentleman has pushed me into naming the paper, I have done so in the terms that I now use. The story is a fabrication.'

The end of the matter is almost too well known to need recounting. The announcement that Pan-American had cancelled its options was made on the day I had said it would be, the last day of the month. An hour later it was followed by an announcement that TWA was cancelling its options also.

The Pan-Am statement said: 'Since [Concorde] has significantly less range, less payload and high operating costs than are provided by current and prospective wide-bodied jets, it will require substantially higher fares than today's. Thus Concorde does not appear to be an airliner that satisfies Pan-Am's future objectives and future requirements as the company now sees them.'

A further paragraph, added at BAC's urgent request, said that Pan-Am would still keep an 'open door' to any later proposals from the makers.

For BAC the 10 days between the *Observer* story and the Pan-Am announcement must have been traumatic. Long before the deadline the BAC sales team had been given Pan-Am's answer. But the makers insisted on their right to make new proposals up to the very last minute. On the final day the Press was called to the Pan-Am executive suite at 3 p.m. It was then kept waiting for two hours while Geoffrey Knight offered almost to give away Concorde. If only Pan-American would extend its options, he said, BAC would explore ways of supporting a purchase in the same way that the British Government had supported the purchase by BOAC. But Pan-Am was adamant. The most it would offer was the face-saving formula about keeping an open door.

The TWA announcement was six weeks ahead of the airline's time limit and totally unexpected. It reached London just as a BAC official was telling reporters that all was not lost and that TWA would now be the focus of the sales campaign.

14. Disaster at Le Bourget

For 18 hours after the American cancellations, announced on the BBC's late-evening news bulletins, the BAC public-relations department was virtually incommunicado. At Bristol it fell to Lew Gray, the Chairman of the shop stewards, to say what the Filton workers were feeling. Nearly all were convinced that the cancellations had been engineered by American aircraft firms. It was useless to explain that the American industry had for months looked to American purchases of Concorde to get the SST programme started again.

BAC finally called a Press conference at four in the afternoon, about the same time that Mr Heseltine was telling the House of Commons that the Government would still give every support to the manufacturers' sales efforts.

The Press assembled at a house in Belgravia to meet a visibly strained George Edwards. Because of the American decision, Concorde production might need to be 'wound down', he said. One way of doing this might be to close one of the production lines. In this way production capacity at one line could be kept in existence for the day when American airlines would have to change their minds because of the success of Concorde with BOAC and Air France.

It was a clever stroke. By making this suggestion and arousing immediate trade-union opposition to it, Sir George denied the Government a possible option, a step towards closing down the programme altogether.

The alternative was to try to string out production at both Bristol and Toulouse over the next two years. To do this would certainly mean building more than the 16 planes so far authorized, of which only 9 were firmly ordered. In short, it would require the Government to commit further funds to production, which would itself add to the 'investment' that must not be thrown away.

The Government kept its counsels to itself, helped by the fact that France was in the throes of a general election and that it was difficult to discuss the next steps until the new French Government was in office.

The election results favoured the Gaullists, but with a much reduced majority. During the campaign the Radical Party, led by Jean-Jacques Servan-Schreiber, made great play of the troubles over Concorde; it was a brave move (Servan-Schreiber spoke personally in Toulouse) but it cost the party votes.

On 13 February, two weeks after the Pan-American and TWA cancellations, six options were dropped by American Airlines. Others followed. Continental Airlines and Belgium's Sabena both cancelled on 29 March. A few hours later the new Australian Government of Mr Whitlam let it be known that it would not approve any QANTAS purchase that could not be justified on commercial grounds and Lufthansa disclosed that on the Frankfurt–New York run Concorde's guaranteed payload capacity was only 61 passengers – well under half the seats allowed for in the design. The next day BAC and Aerospatiale announced that the system of options, binding customers to a decision date, would be ended. The number of options had by now fallen from 72 to 24 and but for the decision to end the system, there is little doubt that most of the remaining option holders would have cancelled before their deadlines.

New troubles were threatening on the other side of the Atlantic. The New York State legislature was considering a Bill which would limit the landing and take-off noise for all aircraft to 108 decibels. An appeal-court decision established that, in case of dispute, the FAA and not the state authorities had the right to fix noise levels. But this merely switched the environmentalists' anti-noise campaign from state to federal level.

There were also signs of a strong attempt to get the American SST relaunched in the next federal budget. During the previous year the administration had spent $70 million on supersonic research. On 16 March Senator Proxmire's committee reported strongly against a revival, but the battle with Seattle was obviously going to continue. If the administration were to back a new design, it could be a development from the cancelled Dash–300. Or it could embody entirely new aerodynamic concepts. Whichever it was, it was bound to have much greater range and capacity than Concorde and would be as worrying to BAC as it was to the environmentalists.

As far as future orders were concerned, everything seemed to depend on Japan Air Lines.

The day after the Pan-Am announcement the JAL president, Mr Shizuo Asada, was reported as saying: 'Japan Air Lines (whose option had a month more to run) has no intention of buying the Concorde'. It was later explained that what he really meant was that there was little possibility of the options being extended. Immediately Aerospatiale dispatched an emergency team. As a result the options were extended to May, and then to the end of the year. If JAL were to confirm orders for three or more Concordes by 31 December, they could still trigger orders, including perhaps American orders, for routes on the Pacific – or so the British Government seemed to hope.

Another country to which Concorde's makers looked hopefully was the Soviet Union, which used the occasion of Aeroflot's 50th anniversary to say that it intended to operate the Tu–144 'whatever happened to Concorde'. The Russians were important to the Concorde in two ways. First, they commanded what was now thought to be the most workable supersonic air route, between London and Tokyo via Moscow and Novosibirsk. Second, the development of the 144 could be cited as evidence that, notwithstanding the rejection of Concorde by Western airlines, the world was on the threshold of a supersonic revolution. After the American cancellations, Britain took up with Russia the question of supersonic traffic rights; and both British and French Ministers made frequent friendly references to Russian aviation technology.

The new *entente* was particularly evident at the next Paris Air Show, in May 1973, which was also used to focus attention on the future of the European aircraft industry and the need to secure world markets.

Once again, as in 1971, the most publicized exhibits at Le Bourget were Concorde and the Tupolev. But this time the

Tu–144 was a very different aeroplane. For the past two years the Tupolev design team had been working on the modifications necessary to improve the plane's performance and particularly its low-speed stability. The most striking modification was the fitting of small retractable foreplanes (canards) behind the flight deck. There was also a basic change in the cross-section of the fuselage which had been lengthened and widened, to provide 140 seats; a movement outboard of the engines; and a change in the design and method of retracting the undercarriage.*

At the Tupolev factory in Voronezh work had gone ahead with the setting up of a production line, said to be for an output of 60-70 aircraft, beginning with an initial Aeroflot order for 30, to be followed by the East German, Czech and Hungarian airlines' orders. Celebrating Aeroflot's 50th anniversary in February, officials had spoken of inaugurating Tu–144 domestic services, mainly between Moscow and Siberia destinations, in 1975, and of starting up international services soon afterwards. But an oblique admission that there were troubles with the Tu–144 was made in March in an article published in the French Press by the Soviet journalist Victor Louis. Writing in *Le Monde,* Louis suggested that France, Britain and the Soviet Union should pool their resources to solve various problems, including those of noise, pollution, and economics, in a second-generation supersonic transport to follow the Tu–144 and Concorde.

In view of the tragedy that occurred later, it should be noted that in addition to facilities at Voronezh, the Russians had an elaborate organization for ground and flight testing the 144. Every new Soviet aircraft, civil or military, must go through the scientific testing institute of the Air Force known as N11 VVS, about 15 miles from Moscow. There is also the Scientific Research Institute of the Ministry of Civil Aviation (N11 GVF), the Flight Testing Institute of the Ministry of Aircraft Production (L11 MAR) and the central Aero-Engine Institute (CIAM). It has been suggested that some of the

*Data for the revised version were: length 216 feet, wing-span 94 feet 6 inches, cruising speed 2,300 km/hr to 2,500 km/hr, maximum range 6,500 km, cruising altitude 52,500-59,000 feet, take-off weight 396,800 lb.

modifications appearing on the Tu–144 at Paris were the result of criticisms of the original design by some of these safety institutes; it has also been suggested that, in their haste to beat Britain and France to the introduction of supersonic services, the Russians went ahead with production of the modified aircraft without completing what, by Anglo–French standards, would have been a full test programme.

The Tu–144 which appeared at Le Bourget was described as a pre-production aircraft, but one so close to the production model that it could be put into service with only small changes. It was flown to Paris by a senior Tupolev test pilot, Mikhail Kozlov, and positioned, like the prototype two years before, close to the Concorde 001. For 11 days it was seen by thousands, inspected inside and out by Western officials, and given generous coverage by the British and French aviation Press which clearly saw it as Concorde's ally, rather than as a rival for sales purposes.

Rivalry persisted, however, and it was probably inevitable that it should take an acute form during the performance demonstrations that are the concluding feature of every Paris *salon*.

There were two main flying displays on the final weekend at Le Bourget. The first, on Saturday 2 June, passed without incident but not altogether without drama. In it, Kozlov, given a ten-minute 'slot' in which to show the Tupolev's paces, seemed determined to recapture the limelight which the Concorde had attracted by regularly flying airline officials and guests during the show.

Following Concorde, which had had a slightly longer demonstration time, he flew the 144 in two low-level passes down the length of the runway and over the heads of 300,000 spectators. The first pass was a straightforward high-speed overflight. The second, much more daring, was at low speed, with canards and landing gear extended. Flying at about 200 m.p.h. Kozlov rolled the plane backwards and forwards at angles of bank of about 45 degrees.

This was something the Concorde had not done. But Kozlov went further. To finish off, he turned the plane 90 degrees for a left-hand approach to runway 03, and came in to land so low and flat that the wheels almost grazed the grass on the runway overrun. Many pilots among the spectators thought Kozlov had made a landing error; others thought he was trying to show the crowd that the canards provided a spectacular degree of low-speed control.

Next day it was again Concorde that flew first, piloted by the Aerospatiale chief test pilot, Jean Franchi. This time, making a slow-speed pass, Franchi imitated Kozlov's trick of the day before, rolling the wings to even sharper bank angles. Then, making a third pass, he brought the plane down till the wheels touched the runway in an on-and-off landing. It was a brilliant, almost provocative performance, which Kozlov must have seen quite clearly as he waited to take off at the end of the runway.

Though the truth will never be known, it would not be surprising if Kozlov had attempted to go one better still. His co-pilot, Valery Molchanov, had provoked speculation about this possibility a few days earlier. Asked about Concorde's performances, Molchanov had told visitors to the 144: 'We have a few tricks. We have more power than the Concorde.'*

As the Concorde turned to park after landing, the Tupolev gathered speed for take-off. It lifted off half way down the runway, climbed to 1,000 feet and turned to make a slow-speed pass, rocking its wings as it had done the day before – but, some spectators thought, more cautiously. It then retracted its canards and landing gear and came round for a second pass. It was not a neat manoeuvre; for some reason the plane had drifted too far south and was obliged to make a further turn to align with the runway. Perhaps Kozlov had become disorientated; perhaps the raised nose-visor impeded his view – there are various explanations.

The Tupolev appeared to prepare for a third pass. But instead of making the usual circle the pilot – possibly realizing that he had used up too much time – made an S-turn that should have brought him more quickly in line with the runway. The landing gear and canards were extended again, the speed reduced and the plane very low. Some spectators thought Kozlov was planning to imitate Concorde's touch-and-go;

* *Aviation Week*, 11 June 1973.

others that he intended a normal landing. But he was too far to the right of the runway.

As he came in, close above the roofs of the chalets where spectators from the aircraft industry were watching, Kozlov switched on the after-burners to climb into circuit again.

The plane rose, as Concorde had done after its touch-and-go manoeuvre 10 minutes before, but perhaps a little more steeply than Concorde. Then just about the point where Concorde had flattened out, observers saw the 144's nose suddenly drop. According to *Aviation Week,* a French engineer said he saw the aircraft yaw (swing sideways) before the nose went down. Other witnesses thought the left wing had dropped first. An experienced pilot shouted: 'He's going in.'

As the 144 went into a steep dive pieces of it appeared to fall off. But it was still largely in one piece when the crew tried to pull out at only 2,000 feet.

Then, as the dive angle flattened slightly, the left wing broke away and the plane rolled onto its back. Next moment the fin came away, perhaps from the stress of the twist; then the right wing, then the droop nose-visor, and a shower of fuselage panels and other fragments.

As the wings snapped off, fires broke out from the severed fuel lines. (Three miles away, to spectators on the airfield, they looked like 'flashing lights'.) Moments later what remained of the aircraft exploded in a fireball as it hit the ground.

The fragments of the plane, plunging into the small suburban community of Goussainville, killed seven people, including several children. All six crew members were also killed, including the chief flight test engineer for the Tu–144 programme, Vladimir Benderov.

The disaster, in full view of the 300,000 spectators at Le Bourget, was a terrible blow for Soviet technology; but its true significance depended on the ability of Russian and French investigators to locate the cause – a task made particularly difficult by their failure to find the relevant portion of the in-flight recorder wire.

There were four possibilities.

First, confusion in the cockpit. This could have occurred if the flight crew had become disorientated by the raising of the visor, or had been trying to catch up on lost time. Or it could have been caused by a system malfunction distracting the crew – though there was no indication of this to the control tower.

Second, a structural failure. Suspicion here rested on the possible failure of one of the canards, which would have been consistent with the violent downward pitch of the aircraft's nose. But there could also have been a break-up in one of the engines. According to *Aviation Week* the Russians had talked to at least one Western visitor about turbine blade problems – and a broken blade or turbine wheel could have damaged the wing or controls.

Third, a flame-out, i.e. sudden cessation of combustion, in one or more engines. This could have been caused by a combination of acceleration forces, the motion of the plane and its attitude at the top of the climb.

Finally there was the possibility that the crew, after igniting the after-burners, found they had too much pitch-up and only marginal forward control force. This would have left them with the choice between continuing an uncontrollable pitch-up with the after-burners on, or shutting the latter off at a critical combination of airspeed and angle of attack (the angle of the plane to its line of flight) and causing a stall.

Such a situation could be described as being caused by a manoeuvre outside the normal 'performance envelope' of a passenger plane, and from a sales point of view would be the least damaging explanation.

The British Government was the quickest to react to the implications of the crash for Concorde. The 144 and the Concorde were two quite different designs, the Aerospace Minister, Mr Heseltine, told the Press the same evening. Concorde would be the most thoroughly tested aircraft in the world.

Yet the fact remained that the Tupolev and the Concorde were both slender delta wing designs. Not only did they *look* similar; they also had common aerodynamic characteristics and had become mutually supporting in their makers' bid to convince the world that the supersonic age was about to begin.

Within 48 hours the Japanese Government said that no supersonic, Anglo–French or Russian, would be permitted to operate from Tokyo without absolute certainty about its safety characteristics. Similar assurances were demanded by anti-Concorde groups in America and other countries. But in Moscow the Soviet Government said that production of the 144 would continue unaffected.

It fell to Bo Lundberg, two months afterwards, to draw the one unassailable conclusion that was possible from the disaster.*

The crash, he said, was no proof that supersonic transports were unsafe. But it did focus attention on the all-important question: could they ever attain the same level of safety as subsonic airliners?

Recalling that ever since 1961 he had warned that SSTs would inevitably be much less safe, Lundberg went on: 'One factor that has contributed to current air-safety levels is that subsonic developments have been an evolutionary process, characterized by just one or two, usually small, technical innovations in each new type of aircraft. On the few occasions when a radically new feature has been introduced, such as the jet engine, other novelties have been avoided. Furthermore the great volume of commercial aviation – about 110 million flights in the last 10 years – has provided enormous service experience.'

In contrast to these solid foundations of subsonic air safety, he saw four main factors combining to reduce the safety of the supersonic transport:

1. It must fly in *two aerodynamic environments,* subsonic and supersonic, with widely different 'laws' in respect of optimum wing shape, stability, etc. Any SST had therefore to be a compromise, inevitably much more complicated than a subsonic jet. Examples of complex novelties in the Tu-144 and Concorde were the delta wing, the pumping of fuel back and forth for balancing the plane when it went supersonic, the droop nose, and the variable air intakes. Such simultaneous innovations increased the risks.

2. The severe *aerodynamic heating* caused by supersonic flight also necessitated novel design features (e.g. using fuel as a cooling agent) and brought an increased risk of failure

* 'Concorde: Unsafe at any Speed?' *Observer*, 5 August 1973.

through metal fatigue. Concorde was being put through impressive tests at Farnborough* intended to simulate the repeated changes of load and temperature to which it would be subjected in service. But this was not enough. Not only did such tests take up to 100 times longer than tests for subsonic structures, with the result that airlines using the first supersonics would not know the outcome of any full-scale test until many years after their SSTs had entered service, but the load and heat pattern that an individual SST would meet in service could be expected to differ significantly from that chosen for the test.

3. There were also novel features in the *operation* of SSTs. For example, subsonic aircraft usually arrived at their destinations with substantial fuel reserves, whereas the SST, with its marginal payload, would usually carry the minimum reserve, which might be encroached upon by unforeseen deviations from the route. Furthermore supersonic flight increased the risk of encountering unforeseen weather conditions, such as clear-air turbulence and clouds containing hail – and the SST's high cruise altitude could mean death to its occupants in the event of a sudden decompression in the cabin.

4. Operating experience with SSTs could never approach the airlines' enormous experience with subsonic transports, which offered no guide to the unique safety problems of the SST. And although Concorde, with its many novelties, might be – in the makers' words – 'the most tested plane in the history of aviation', testing could only minimize the *foreseeable* risks; it could not remove the unpredictable ones. It was the unpredictable coincidence of several causes that produced most disasters, and the probability of such coincidences rose rapidly with the number of simultaneous innovations.

* The Farnborough tests, which began in 1972, involve the use of a multi-million-pound 'torture chamber' containing a complete airframe. By compressing the effect of two 3,500-mile, 3½ hour flights into the space of an hour, and by continuing day and night without interruption, they are intended to be capable of predicting within 10 years that Concorde has at least a 15-year life span. See Society of British Aerospace Companies, *News Letter*, 12 August 1971.

All this should be enough to deter passengers, as well as agencies which might contemplate building, operating or indeed, insuring SSTs, said Lundberg. But supersonic safety must also be seen in the perspective of aviation safety as a whole. This had to be continuously improved. For if aviation safety were threatening to stagnate again, as it had from 1953 to 1961, the number of passengers killed would increase as rapidly as aviation itself.

Taking the 1971-2 average of 1,550 deaths per year as a basis, unimproved safety plus a 10 per cent annual traffic growth would result in over 10,000 deaths a year in 20 years' time – or about one major disaster a day, which would be fatal for confidence in aviation.

In view of all this, what could possibly justify the introduction of the SST with all its risks, asked Lundberg? – 'The only noteworthy benefit, to a tiny minority, is the cutting of a few hours from long journeys, a gain that will often be pointless, since it usually takes several *days* to adjust to a new local time. And the price of this gain, apart from operating losses, will be the SST's severe ground noise and the creation of the sonic boom . . .'

Postscript

As this book goes to press, eight months after the American cancellations, there is a tendency on the part of its opponents to 'write off' Concorde. This is premature if by 'writing off' is meant the cancellation of the Anglo–French programme. Enough has happened in 13 years to show that political pressures can keep the programme going long after the last vestige of an economic argument for its continuation has been exploded.

But equally, with the recent revision of its sales prospects, it is right to draw up a balance sheet showing what has been achieved and what squandered, and to try to identify the rea-

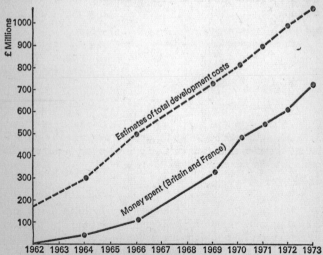

Figure 15. Concorde costs and spending.

sons for this folly, which is possibly the greatest in the history of civil technology.

A serious attempt at part of this task was made in 1973 by the House of Commons Committee of Public Accounts. On 27 July the Committee reported on evidence taken three months earlier from senior officials involved in the project. In the published proceedings* there were nearly 100 excisions of figures which the Government had asked to be withheld for reasons of commercial security. This made parts of the Report difficult to understand and drew from the Committee the comment that the Government 'should seriously consider whether the confidentiality they have demanded for so much of the information about this project is in fact in the public interest'. Nevertheless, enough remained to substantiate the Committee's very considerable criticism of the way the project had been handled.

The absence of any clear indication of both sales prospects and the general level of production if sales were low, left the Concorde project 'as speculative as it ever was', said the Report. And unless further substantial orders were received, it was likely that in addition to a failure to recover development costs the Government would have to meet production losses 'which could be large on each aircraft produced'.

The Committee made no recommendation about continuing or cancelling the project, since this would have been beyond its terms of reference; but it was deeply critical of the terms of the Anglo–French collaborative agreement. It questioned

whether in future, and in the light of the Concorde experience, governments should be willing to deprive themselves of all unilateral discretion as to their continued involvement in projects, the cost of which might rapidly escalate above target

and suggested that

perhaps some reconciliation can be found between the conflicting demands of genuine national commitment to international collaboration in advanced technology on the one hand, and the need to retain some national discretion about the extent of involvement in particular projects on the other, by defining dates at which an option can be exercised unilaterally if certain criteria of cost or of performance cannot be met.

* *Sixth and Seventh Reports from the Committee of Public Accounts* House of Commons Paper 335, HM Stationery Office.

In other words, if it had not been for the French connection, Britain should have pulled out of Concorde long before.

The Committee's main concern was with costs, and their escalation from £150–70 million in November 1962 (of which the UK share was put at £75–85 million) to £1,065 million in June 1973 (of which the UK share was put at £525 million). It pointed out that this covered research and development over 13 years to the intended point of certification in 1975, but also that £1,065 would not be the final figure, because the manufacturers were now studying a number of possible improvements which, if approved, would be additional to the current estimate.

A breakdown of costs given in the Report showed that of the total increase of £895 million, only £307 million could be attributed to inflation and changes in exchange rates. The rest (see Figure 16) was caused by programme slippage, revisions

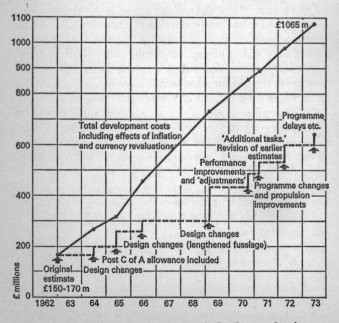

Figure 16. Development costs – how and why they escalated.

of estimates, 'additional development tasks', and other adjustments.

It was also disclosed that at the time of the Committee's hearings just £702 million of the total £1,065 million had been spent. This confirmed the curious trend (see Figure 15) observable ever since 1964 for the final estimate always to be about £300 million ahead of current expenditure.

The Committee unearthed a disparity, hitherto overlooked, between British and French spending on the programme. Britain, it turned out, had spent £371 million and France only £331 million. (Of the British share £215 million had been on work by BAC and £156 million on work by Rolls-Royce; in France £227 million had been spent on work by Aerospatiale, and £104 million on work by SNECMA.) Although contributions were supposed to be equal, the Committee revealed that there was no sure arrangement for adjusting any difference at the end of the day.

More interesting still was the Report's disclosures about the method of calculating the manufacturers' profits on the scheme. (Since 1968, it appeared BAC had made an annual average investment of some £8 million, compared with the Government's £78 million, but the profit referred to was an incentive payment across the whole programme.)

In 1968 the Ministry of Technology had negotiated revised contract terms under which the profit payable within defined limits would depend on the cost out-turn and on the payload achieved, as compared with agreed cost and payload targets. Lower costs and higher payloads would increase the profit payable to BAC and vice versa.

The arrangements provided for full reimbursement of all costs reasonably incurred and a minimum profit, and allowed for adjustment of the target cost for changes in the levels of wages and prices and 'for certain specified changes in the work programme'. The first target was determined by taking BAC's estimates of total costs to Certificate of Airworthiness, deducting from this the expenditure hitherto (April 1968) and then adding 15 per cent for contingencies.

Since the Government was bearing the main risk in the programme, the rate of profit at the target point was fixed lower than was the case with most other government contracts. But the Committee noted that 'the incentive to reduce costs diminished as costs rose to the level at which the minimum profit operated and disappeared when that level was reached'.

As a result, once costs exceeded 115 per cent of the target (which they had done, and more) BAC could only increase its profits by improving the payload, for which a variable profit was payable over a range of 18,000 lb. to 25,000 lb. Thus, in the words of the Committee, 'the arrangements were likely to have ceased to act as any significant incentive to keep costs down and, in fact, could encourage BAC to try to persuade the Government to spend more money to improve performance so that the Company's profits would be greater'.

After regretting the lack of incentives to economy and efficiency, the Report went on: 'We note that the Ministry are hoping to negotiate fixed prices for as much as possible for the remaining development work. However, little more than half the remaining work on the airframe and even less on the engine will lend itself to fixed price contracts, even in a form modified to take account of remaining technical uncertainties.'

The big question left open by the Committee's report, because of the Government's 'commercial' censorship, was the exact amount of the loss to be expected on production. This was excised from the minutes of evidence. However, a member of the Committee, Mr Reginald Paget QC, subsequently gave his private opinion that, even in the most favourable circumstances (i.e. without any break in production) and assuming a price substantially above that paid by BOAC, the average loss on a run of 30 aircraft would be £5-8 million per aircraft sold, and that losses would continue until about the 60th aircraft.

Another vital figure censored in the published minutes – the amount of the research and development levy to be made on each sale – could be deduced from a report published three months before by the Public Accounts Committee's French counterpart, the Cour des Comptes.

Making no less serious criticisms of the French side of the

Concorde programme (and incidentally revealing a tip of the great French Treasury opposition to the project), the Cour des Comptes disclosed that 'according to the responsible authorities' 300 Concordes would have to be sold to recover the research and development investment.

From this it could be calculated that the R and D levy per aircraft would be about £3.5 million – and also, with the help of one of the few figures that slipped uncensored into the PAC Report (an answer to a question on the proposition of the R and D costs likely to be recovered), that the British Government was still hoping for a sale of 60-90 Concordes to bring a recovery of 20-30 per cent.

From all that has been said in the preceding chapters – about Concorde's operating costs, its colossal sales price, its payload and range limitations, the uncertainties about its routes, its noise and boom problem, and, not least, doubts about its passenger appeal – it should be clear that these sales estimates, which were made before the American cancellations, are, to put it mildly, absurdly optimistic.

It is true that, if and when Concorde enters service with BOAC and Air France, it may achieve high load factors on one or two routes because of the two airlines' supersonic monopoly. Indeed, it will have to in order to cover even part of its cost. But other, non-subsidized airlines know only too well that such load factors will be the product of a highly artificial situation.

They also know that, if any substantial number of airlines were to order supersonics, all would end up by paying much higher costs in order to carry the same volume of passengers as before. (In this event the operating loss would be passed to ordinary *sub*sonic passengers, who would thus contribute still further to subsidize the supersonic 'jet set'.)

The alternative is for the airlines to continue investing in the latest subsonics, which will not only be safer and more comfortable, but also, in the case of the new Special Performance Boeing 747 (with a non-stop range of 6,500 miles) capable of covering long distances almost as fast as Concorde, which has to stop to refuel.

In the summer of 1973 this was clearly most airlines' inten-

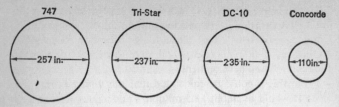

| 747 | Tri-Star | DC-10 | Concorde |

Figure 17. Passenger comfort – comparative cabin widths.

tion; and if Bo Lundberg is right,* the economics of supersonic flight confronting them will not be greatly changed by the offer of any larger design. This is because any increase in capacity must be accompanied by an increase in gross weight, with the result that the payload-to-weight ratio – the most important factor in a plane's economics – will remain substantially the same.

But suppose (it may be asked) the airlines led by short-sighted competitive instincts, or coerced by their governments for prestige reasons into changing their minds; what will happen?

The consequences will be twofold.

First, because of the delays and miscalculations in Concorde's design and development the beneficiary will not be Concorde but an American successor, which will take over the field as the Boeing 707 took over the field from the Comet. Second, unless there is some quite radical breakthrough in technology, e.g. to eliminate the boom, the nightmare of environmental pollution, which has temporarily receded because of the SST's cancellation and Concorde's sales failure, will be revived with a vengeance.

Certainly there will be scant respect by either governments or operators for the dangers of upper-atmosphere pollution, which cannot be clarified without many more years of work. And one cannot suppose that governments with an interest

* In evidence to the Sub-Committee on Priorities and Economy in Government, Joint Economic Committee of Congress, 27 December 1972. See Record of Hearings, US Government Printing Office, Washington, DC, Stock Number 5270-01743. The Record contains Lundberg's detailed mathematical demonstration of his argument.

in supersonic manufacture will long resist pressure to boost sales by permitting supersonic overflights.

To prevent the possibility of this situation developing, Lundberg has proposed two courses of action: that the airlines, which would stand to lose heavily from enforced supersonic operations, should get together to secure a reaffirmation of IATA's 'ten commandments' regarding an acceptable supersonic design; and that governments and organizations with environmental interests should work for a declaration on the Supersonic Transport by the UN Environment Council.

But urgently desirable though these moves may be, the prime opportunity for restoring sense to commercial aviation development rests with the British and French Governments.

The full cost of their commitment to Concorde is now all too plain. It only *begins* with the £1,065 million development cost estimate, which, on the Government's own admission, is likely to be increased by a further large sum for noise improvement.

To this must be added production losses, amounting, on the evidence of Mr. Paget (who has not been contradicted), to about £6 million per plane on the most optimistic sales estimate, plus the likely non-return of the greater part of a £250-350 million production loan for which authority was sought and received from Parliament.

But this is not all. The total costs also include the £130 million 'public dividend' capital given to BOAC, which is unlikely to yield interest in the foreseeable future.

Taking in similar sums that must certainly have been spent or committed on the French side, the total joint bill for Concorde could thus be upward of £2,000 million – Britain's share being slightly over half because of BOAC's fifth Concorde (Air France has bought only four) and the probable non-rectification of the £40 million difference in development spending discovered by the Public Accounts Committee.

Of this colossal sum, only about £900 million has so far been spent (about £475 million of it by Britain), so that by stopping the programme *now* the Government could make a saving far in excess of any sum needed for the re-settlement of the 25,000 British workers engaged on Concorde.

The gains achieved by all this expenditure, not just of money but of the skills and resources for which money stands, are meagre to the point of being negligible.

The greatest gain might be thought to be political. Concorde has helped to buy Britain's ticket of entry into Europe. But no one could now pretend that a speculative supersonic aircraft was the best way to secure France's friendship. On the contrary, Britain's adherence to a discredited venture for fear of offending General de Gaulle created a false relationship whose consequences are still being felt.

It is sometimes claimed that Concorde has been indispensable to the maintenance of British advanced technology. This too is exaggerated. What in fact has happened is that the concentration of resources on Concorde has starved other sectors of British industry, including sectors of the aircraft industry, with the result that in fields where Britain held the lead, such as vertical take-off, she has fallen behind.

Nor, except in the form of our ability to make further uneconomic supersonic transports, has there been any siginificant 'fall out' from the Concorde programme.

What we are left with is an elegant but environmentally 'dirty' aeroplane, capable of transporting a limited number of people twice as fast as any previous aircraft but totally without prospects commercially.

In the autumn of 1973 there could be no doubt that the whole supersonic adventure, in both Britain and America (and, on any analysis, in Russia as well), has been an enormous fiasco. If it has achieved anything, it is simply this:

It has shown that in the nature of things there can never be a 'cost estimate' for a project at the frontiers of knowledge.

It has shown that advanced technological projects that cannot be justified on their own merits make poor vehicles for international collaboration.

It has shown the tremendous political stupidity of concealing the facts and difficulties of such a programme from Parliament.

But the main lesson is more positive:

It has also shown that, although modern society remains

obsessed with technological playthings, there is a growing body of opinion, in the West at least, that has passed through adolescence and is prepared to fight for a sane order of social and technological priorities.

Appendix

IATA Requirements for the Supersonic Airliner, 1962

Safety: The level of safety afforded by the SST must be at least equal to that of subsonic aircraft operating at the time it is introduced into service. This implies that:

1 – Cabin structural integrity must be assured, since the possibility of rapid decompression in flight cannot be tolerated.

2 – Good aircraft control response and handling characteristics are essential to safe operation. They are important at all speeds but particularly in the low-speed régime. Control response and handling characteristics of the SST must therefore be comparable to, or better than, those of subsonic aircraft.

3 – There must be a vast improvement over existing materials, structures, systems and instruments prior to introduction of the SST into airline service. Only thus can the necessary standards of reliability and maintainability be achieved. Only thus can the desired airframe life of at least 30,000 hours be attained and satisfactory overall reliability be extended.

4 – Thorough flight testing of one or more prototype aircraft is required under airline operating conditions. This must be carried out before the production programme of an SST is launched if safe operation is to result, if serious errors are to be avoided, and if the costly period of change normally experienced with new equipment is to be eliminated.

Compatibility: The SST must be adaptable to air traffic control facilities existing at the time of its introduction into service so that it is capable of integration with subsonic aircraft operating at that time.

This means that:

5 – Runway length and strength requirements for the SST must be no greater than those for large subsonic jets operating at that time.

6 – SST flight characteristics in the airport terminal area, such as speed, glide slope, and holding patterns, should permit its treatment as 'just another aircraft' without undue penalty. The SST must be capable of mixing with other traffic in all weather.

Efficiency: The SST must be competitive with subsonic aircraft operating at the time of its introduction. *Accordingly:*

7 – No increase in the level of engine noise can be tolerated. In fact, engine noise from the SST must be lower than that of subsonic jets operating at present in order to permit round-the-clock operations.

8 – Economic operations at supersonic speed must be practicable over inhabited areas at any time of the day or night. Sonic boom could prevent this unless the aircraft is designed to permit practical and economic operating procedures for its alleviation.

9 – SST – seat mile costs must be equal to or better than those of subsonic jets of comparable size and range operating at the time of its introduction.

10 – The SST must be capable of reasonably economic operation at subsonic speeds as a considerable portion of its operation will be at the slower speeds. Its design should permit this without unduly penalizing its supersonic performance.

More about Penguins and Pelicans

Penguinews, which appears every month, contains details of all the new books issued by Penguins as they are published. From time to time it is supplemented by *Penguins in Print*, which is a complete list of all available books published by Penguins. (There are well over four thousand of these.)

A specimen copy of *Penguinews* will be sent to you free on request. For a year's issues (including the complete lists) please send 30p if you live in the United Kingdom, or 60p if you live elsewhere. Just write to Dept EP, Penguin Books Ltd, Harmondsworth, Middlesex, enclosing a cheque or postal order, and your name will be added to the mailing list.

Note: *Penguinews* and *Penguins in Print* are not available in the U.S.A. or Canada

Poverty: The Forgotten Englishman

Ken Coates and Richard Silburn

Is poverty in Britain a thing of the past? Too many of our countrymen regularly do without the minimum considered necessary for a healthy diet; they live in houses that are overcrowded, insanitary and ludicrously expensive to keep warm and comfortable; their children attend schools in which teaching is a near-impossibility.

Ken Coates and Richard Silburn look again at what is meant by the word 'poverty'. They conclude that vast numbers of Englishmen, living in slums throughout the country, are, for most of their lives, living in acute poverty. What this actually involves is spelled out by means of a detailed survey of one slum – St Ann's, an area of Nottingham which has now been cleared but remains typical of hundreds of such districts.

The book continues with a study of welfare services and why they fail to alleviate or remove poverty, and finally there is an analysis of the frequent failure of slum-clearance schemes.

Originally published as a Penguin Special, this Pelican attacks a problem – that of modern urban poverty – neglected by western society.

'Writing with compassion, style, wit and an almost complete lack of jargon, (they) present us with inescapable facts which must remould our thinking and our actions' – *The Times*